Here is a for you.

C000078808

ISBN 978-1-909797-43-7

To Avril
Ironically there are no words that can
truly express the gift you gave me. I hope this book,
and the others that follow, will explain to the world,
what you taught me. Our role is not to control our
mind, but to be curious, make friends with it
and enjoy the journey.

REVIEWS

"Helen beautifully **weaves together insights and practical tips for aligning your mindset and actions, to your business aspirations.** Not just in relation to money but also other aspects of business such as marketing too. Through **gently encouraging you to question your beliefs and habits,** Helen guides you on **a thought-provoking journey of self-reflection.** She writes with the same **wisdom and warmth** that I enjoy in our conversations. By reading this book you'll have **a better conscious awareness of what's holding you back,** and **plenty of ideas** for what you can do to put yourself in the best place to succeed."

Alisoun Mackenzie, The Compassionate Marketing Mentor, Speaker & Author of Heartatude – The 9 Principles Of Heart-Centered Success

"**Successful Business Minds is an excellent resource for anyone** either considering starting a business or anyone who is running a business and feeling stuck and unable to move forward. One of the biggest challenges any business person will tell you that they face is that of **keeping a positive mindset** and ensuring that we have the personal resilience to keep going when things get tough and this can be the **difference between success or failure.** Running a business can be lonely and keeping the mind in a healthy place can be a greater challenge than bringing in the sales.

I love the way **Helen has used her insight** of hypnotherapy and NLP, blended it with her own **wealth of knowledge** in accounting and applied it to business **to help individuals to fully align their thinking** when it comes to running a business.

Being self-employed and running a business is way more than having a business plan and turning a profit and with Helen's insight and business knowledge in this book she **helps the reader to understand** the importance of aligning the conscious, unconscious and creative part of our mind to **be fully present and aligned as an entrepreneur.** Thus enabling us to **engage with our business and customers authentically** and in alignment with who we are - to **develop a healthy, successful business mindset,** which after all is **where all our business success will ultimately flow from.**"

Avril Gill, Hypnotherapy & NLP Trainer, Newlands Personal Development

"When I sat down to read this book I couldn't put it down. As an accountant whose own business helps others, I am always searching ways to help businesses thrive. **Successful Business Minds cleverly covers what it takes to have a successful business and be happy!** Broken into easy to read sections, with takeaways from each chapter, this book will help you on your journey. **I took action immediately after reading the book.** Highly recommended. **This is my new go-to book for both myself and as a resource for my clients.**"

Michelle Gregory, ACMA, Gregory Accounting

"Successful Business Minds is a thought-provoking guide for purpose-led business owners who want to serve others AND create a sustainable business. In her book, Helen shares **simple strategies and mindset tips** to **help business owners** to **rethink their relationship with money.** With practical steps and real life examples, this is **THE book you need** if you're ready to **improve your relationship with money, attract more clients and make more profit,** whilst providing an exceptional service to your clients."

Karen Williams, The Book Mentor, Librotas

Successful Business Minds **is a well-written and very informative book** *for readers seeking* **practical guidance and intuitive help** *with improving their relationship with money, and* **achieving greater happiness through alignment of your head, heart, body and soul.** *The author, Helen Monaghan is clearly a non-stereotypical management accountant and finance coach whose experience clearly shines throughout. Her blended knowledge in finance, NLP, hypnotherapy and well-assembled accounts of clients' stories is beautifully packaged. Successful Business Minds supplies a holistic view of how our attitudes and* **behaviours formed as far back as childhood,** *impact our values.* **Our perception about money influences the decisions we** *make in our business and life, which can* **bring us closer to or take us further away from achieving our desired success.** *As a Solopreneur Business Coach who leads with a success mindset principle,* **I concur 100% with Helen's reference to,** **"You need to make friends with your mind for your business to be successful."**. *The cases studies and practical exercises presented are particularly helpful and give readers a lovely down-to-earth feeling. The top takeaways from each chapter serve as an added bonus and excellent summary and reflection points.* **"Do you love yourself enough to look after your finances"**, *is a real eye-opener' which challenges you to* **think much deeper** *than you've probably given consideration to before. If you're thinking of starting a business, you are already in business, or simply looking for ways to seriously improve your relationship with money, you're in for a real treat! I highly recommend you read Successful Business Minds. It's* **your personal life coach** *for a small fee* **with a BIG return** *that will serve you a lifetime, as you transition through every stage in life and journey towards your desired success.*

Beverley Anderson, The Solopreneur Business Accelerator, BusinessBoostExperts

Successful Business Minds is **a refreshing read.** *Finally, an accountant that gets no matter how much you tell me I need to make a profit I cannot act unless* **it 'feels' right.** *A practical and* **lovingly written book** *that I believe will inspire heart centred businesses not only to survive but thrive. Which has to be a good thing. We all need to be supported at difficult times in our life and those that run holistic businesses often do at the expense of their own health and family.* **This book will not only inspire you to charge what you are worth** *but also to* **value your time.** *I would also like to think that it could also inspire other kinds of businesses to become more heart centred.*

Sheryl Andrews, The Strength and Solution Detective, Step by Step Listening

ACKNOWLEDGEMENTS

This book would not have been possible without the support and encouragement from all my friends, family, business associates, clients, fellow authors and authors to be. Most of them have listened to me talk about writing books for years and every one of them encouraged me and believed in me. That is the best gift any potential author could have - that and notebooks and pens!

In particular I would like to express my deep gratitude to Doug, my partner, for his continuous encouragement for my passion to write as well as count; Margaret Ward, my assistant, for helping me to run my business whilst I wrote this book; Mary Turner Thomson, my editor, from WhiteWater Publishing Ltd, for introducing me to the world of publishing and her valuable support throughout writing this book; Lorraine Murray, my reiki trainer, from Connected Kids Ltd, for helping reconnect me to my soul and believing in me when I did not; Alisoun Mackenzie, my authenticity coach, from Alisoun Ltd, for the inspiration & encouragement to write about bringing our heart into our business and being authentic; Avril Gill, my hypnotherapy trainer, from Newlands Personal Development, for giving me the wonderful mind tools that enabled me to make my dream of being an author go from impossible to possible: and finally Karen Williams, my book mentor, from Librotas, for helping me to make this book a reality.

TABLE OF CONTENTS

ABOUT THE AUTHOR

FOREWORD BY ALISOUN MACKENZIE

INTRODUCTION

PART 1 - *FORGET EVERYTHING YOU HAVE BEEN TOLD OR EXPERIENCED ABOUT MONEY*

PART 2 - *WHAT DOES SUCCESS REALLY MEAN FOR YOU?*

PART 3 - *DO YOU FEEL WORTHY OF SUCCESS?*

PART 4 - *DO YOU ACT IN ACCORDANCE TO YOUR SUCCESS OR ARE YOU AFRAID?*

PART 5 - *INTEGRATION AND FURTHER RESOURCES (BEST PRACTICES, TIME MANAGEMENT AND MARKETING)*

ABOUT THE AUTHOR

Helen is a Chartered Management Accountant and BIH accredited NLP Practitioner and Hypnotherapist who runs a successful Finance Coaching practice in Scotland, where she helps businesses and individuals have a better relationship with money, themselves and others.

Helen's passion for finance and psychology was born when she was ten years old. Through her own experience she saw how big an influence money has on our lives, and took charge of her own financial destiny by working weekends whilst still at primary school; always asking 'Why do people do the things they do?'

She encouraged her family and friends to have a better relationship with money so they could take charge of their lives. Then aged 17 years old, whilst she was still in high school, she demonstrated to her part-time employers that she was capable of managing their café in a small parachute centre. Helen later studied accountancy at Stirling University whilst still running the café although she then went on to supervise a much larger operation.

After graduating in 1996, she devoted all her attention to qualifying as a professional chartered management accountant whilst she progressed rapidly through finance management roles. In 2005 after qualifying, she launched her own accountancy business part-time, whilst still working full-time in strategic level finance.

In 2011 Helen trained as a NLP (Neuro-Linguistic-Programming) Practitioner, then shortly afterwards left full-time employment so that she could dedicate her attention to her own business combining finance and NLP. In 2014 she trained as a hypnotherapist and embarked on a six-year journey to study a psychology degree part-time through The Open University to further cement and add credibility to her psychological knowledge.

Helen believes that to achieve a successful business and have a successful life you need to understand yourself and those around you. Her books show you how to do that.

FOREWORD BY ALISOUN MACKENZIE

It breaks my heart, when I meet wonderfully talented and kind-hearted souls, who have set up in business but are not generating enough profit to pay themselves a good salary. Many set off on a quest to turn their passion into a business, with the desire to help and make a difference to others. By setting up as a business one of their intentions has been to make money (or they would have simply volunteered their services), yet many struggle to generate enough cash saying things like:

- *"Money isn't important"*
- *"I don't feel comfortable charging for my services"*
- *"I'm not doing this to make lots of money"*
- *"I want to help those who need my help the most"*
- *"I don't expect to earn as much as I did in the corporate world"*

Then they wonder why they don't have any money!
Can you relate to any of this?

Money doesn't make us happy. However, a lack of it often causes unnecessary stress, worry, anxiety, frustration, disappointment and many arguments. You don't have to choose between money, happiness and being kind. Imagine how different the world could be if we rewarded those doing good, more than those only seeking to line their own pockets ...

I greatly admire those who are motivated to make a difference, improve the lives of others or to share a valuable message. These are lovely qualities, but having a kind heart isn't enough to succeed in business. Neither is being brilliant at what you do, nor learning all the best marketing strategies in the world. Making a profit (for personal or social gain) is what differentiates a business from an expensive hobby. What would you prefer?

Your relationships with money, success and your own self-worth all determine how profitable your business will be. If you are nurturing any negative beliefs, emotional triggers, behaviours or habits in relation to these you will be sabotaging your success.

The good news is that it IS possible for you to earn good money doing what you love – if you're open to the possibility that you deserve it! You are already a wonderful human being with so much untapped potential and the ability to learn whatever you need to manifest this. I can assure you that when you align your thoughts, feelings and actions in relation to money, to what's important to you, you will enjoy more financial prosperity.

I love Helen's unique perspective on growing a profitable business – blending a heart-centred approach to work with good professional practices that come from being a management accountant (or CPA if you're in North America).

In this book Helen beautifully weaves together insights and practical tips for aligning your mindset and actions to your business aspirations. Not just in relation to money but also other aspects of business such as marketing too.

Through gently encouraging you to question your beliefs and habits, Helen guides you on a thought-provoking journey of self-reflection. She writes with the same wisdom and warmth that I enjoy in our conversations.

By reading this book you'll have a better conscious awareness of what's holding you back, and plenty of ideas for what you can do to put yourself in the best place to succeed.

It's been an absolute honour and delight to have been part of Helen's journey in finding her authentic voice, and birthing this book: *Successful Business Minds*. Helen and this book are gorgeous gifts to the world!

Enjoy!

Alisoun Mackenzie
The Compassionate Marketing Mentor,
Speaker & Author of *Heartatude, The 9 Principles Of Heart-Centered Success*
www.alisoun.com

INTRODUCTION

"Success: the accomplishment of an aim or purpose."
(Oxford English Dictionary)

Does money make you happy, or not?

Some people believe that money makes them happy. They are neither right nor wrong. In fact, it's their perception of what money means to them that will determine what makes them feel joy. The way I look at money is that it enables us to buy something. That could be a house, a car, clothes, holidays, or lunch with a friend. Whatever it is, it is something that is usually out of our reach without money. Not everything can be bought though. Love and sunshine are natural elements of this world and their certainty can never be guaranteed; with or without money. Money could buy the people you love gifts, or time to spend with them, but it does not buy their love. Money buys a holiday in the sun but nature will determine whether or not you actually get sunshine.

What has this to do with a successful business?

Are you familiar with the phrases *'cash is king'* and *'money makes the world go round'*? It is these sayings along with *'money doesn't make you happy'* that cause conflict in your mind when you are running a business. Most business owners strive for profit, yet their subconscious (that is the part of you that acts or thinks without you consciously knowing about it) tells them that will not make them happy. They either sabotage all efforts to make their business successful, or they take a run at it fuelled with their passion only to crash and burn a few years later, exhausted and unhappy.

As an accountant, it is my role to remind you that money does play an important part in running a business. However, there is a lot more to having a successful business that just money. In this book I will discuss and show by example, why a truly successful business can only be achieved through aligning five key elements together:

Logic, Passion, Meaning, Health and Action

Surprisingly, most people do know this but they fail due to the internal battle that occurs over these five elements, and the unconscious beliefs they have.

Many business owners who come to me for finance coaching are kind hearted people who want to make money in their business yet they are struggling to pay their bills. Most of them also have a sickly feeling every time they tell people how much they charge. They tell me that they have reduced their prices when they are not getting sales, which then leads to frustration with how many hours they have to work. This is often time away from their family or friends. It can affect their health and make them question their purpose in life. They may even start to believe that they are meant to express their gift to the world for free.

What if I told you, you could have a successful business; paying your bills, spending time with your family/friends, doing things you love doing and still feel connected to your purpose.

Do you believe this is possible?

Some of my clients think I am kidding them when I tell them they can make a profit. This is proven within two sessions after we review their accounts and I show them how it is possible. Quite simply it is just a matter of looking through their costs, asking what outgoings they cannot do without, then working out how many hours they want to spend in their business. That gives us their minimum price. It is often an eye opener for many business owners by itself. This is an exercise that is frequently forgotten about as many people base their prices on what other people charge.

Once you know what you should be charging for your services/products and assess what the best area to focus on is (ie the most profitable), we then hit one, or all four blocks to success and this is what the rest of our sessions are on, and hence what this book details.

So what are the 4 key challenges to success?

1. What you currently think about money
2. What you currently think about success
3. How much you currently believe you are worthy of success/money
4. Being afraid to take action

People have these challenges because they have not aligned their four minds (metaphorically speaking). Any action you take in your business, and your life, must come from a decision that is harmony with your cognitive mind (head), your emotional mind (heart), your somatic mind (body) and your intuitive mind (soul).

Think of it like four children under your care all wanting to do different things. If you want any peace, you need to negotiate and reason with them. You need to get them all in agreement or you are going to be in for a pretty rough ride! If you have ever been in a company board meeting with directors and shareholders, it can be uncannily similar to this. The only difference being is that in comparison children are often better behaved!

"Although you have a single identity, you're not of a single mind; instead you are a collection of many competing drives."

David Eagleman, neuroscientist, The Brain, The Story of You.

The four minds explained

Our brain is a very thirsty organ (it uses 25% of our energy) and it will take short cuts to preserve that energy. There is lot that goes on in there that even neuroscientists are still trying to work out. However, thanks to psychologists, we do know that your brain is in a constant battle with itself especially when it comes to decision making. The winner is quite simply the strongest neural pathway. The scientists talk about it in a far more complex language than I do here and if you would like to read their material I have included some great resources at the back of this book. For the sake of simplicity however, and because it is much easier to learn when something is explained metaphorically, I talk about the four key drivers of the mind (all those competing drives of yourself) being the **head (Cognitive Mind)**, the **heart (Emotional Mind)**, the physical capability of the **body (Somatic Mind)**, and your **soul (Intuitive Mind)**.

The Four Minds

Cognitive	Emotional	Somatic	Intuitive
⇕	⇕	⇕	⇕
Head (logic)	Heart	Body	Soul
Thoughts	Emotions	Health	Purpose
Decisions	Feelings	Physical Capability	Spirituality
Money Making	Passion	Mental Health	Sense of Self

What you need to know is that when you sense a misalignment such as a discomfort or challenges in your life, you need to stop what you are doing and hold a meeting with your four minds. If everything is going swimmingly well then you know your minds are in agreement and happy, for now.

For example, when you are emotional about something (upset or passionate), your body will be in full agreement with the emotion because it is sensing pain or joy. Before you have had a moment to register what is going on consciously, you find yourself having said something or done something. Shortly after (sometimes milliseconds after) you sense your cognitive mind standing with its mouth wide open in utter shock asking *"What the heck was all that about?!"*

Or perhaps, you have thought something was a good idea and have been incredibly passionate about it (your cognitive and emotional mind are in total agreement) but half way through your body is screaming *"What on earth are you doing to me?!"*

How do I align my four minds so I can have a successful business?

By holding a meeting of the minds for any action that you wish to take in your business, and only taking action when they are in full agreement. Your meeting's agenda will always be asking:

- What does your logical mind want to do about this? Why?
- What do you feel about this? Why?
- Is your body capable of doing this?
- What does your soul say about this?
- Then they are all given the opportunity to respond to the other's statement.

I have a checklist in the resources section and you can download a pdf version from my website by signing up to Successful Business Minds resources at:
www.hmcoaching.co.uk/successful-business-minds-resources

I encourage you to read this book from beginning to end to get the maximum benefit. However, I am aware you may want to refer back to a specific section at a later date, or jump straight to your main challenge right now, in which case I have split it into five parts. The first four parts address the main four challenges with part five being an integration and further resource section to help you get creative with the decisions that your Meeting of the Minds may want to agree on.

In part one I urge you to forget everything you have been told or experienced about money. Forget any negative experiences of money. Forget everything anyone has ever told you about how to achieve money. Forget all the long hours and pain that you experienced whilst attaining money in the past. Forget all the negative comments people and the media have ever said about rich people or any experiences you have had with those who are considered wealthy. We will then look at what money can actually do with the right mindset and behaviour. Money is not, nor ever has been, the problem. It is what people do with money that determines whether it is a good thing or not, and I show you just how important money is to a business.

In part two we will consider what you really want out of life and how your business can give you that. I suggest that you forget all the long hours and pain that you experienced whilst achieving success in the past and be open to thinking that success could come more easily to you. I then ask you to consider what success would really mean for you? Is it money? Is it freedom to choose or is it being at peace? Or maybe it is being allowed to be creative, helping others, or maybe it is something more personal. I encourage you to define what success really means to you. What would it look like? What would it feel like? What would it sound like? How will you recognise it?

In part three I ask you whether or not you feel worthy of success and wealth. Do you deserve a successful business that is making money and helping others whilst you enjoy your life, or are you beating yourself up because you have not learnt the act of self-love?

In part four, we look at the fear behind your actions. Are you self-sabotaging your success or are you truly aligned with achievement? Is every decision you make aligned with your **head, heart, body, and soul**. If not, why not? What are you doing that tells you it is not? Why are you doing that? Are you afraid to make changes? Are you afraid it will change who you are?

Sometimes, not taking action, is simply a matter of not actually knowing what behaviours are appropriate to your success which is why I have included part five as well as a few examples throughout the book. **In part five**, I give suggestions that have worked for my clients and me. They may or may not be a good fit for each of your four minds but they should at least spark a train of thought that will help you find the best strategy that works for you. I have also included a link to a couple of meditation audios that will help you to get creative in your board meeting and identify courses of action in addition to the **Meeting of the Minds agenda**. I also include a list of resources if you would like to find out more information about anything I have written about.

Please note that all client names have been changed to protect client confidentiality.

PART 1

*Forget everything you have been told
or experienced about money*

WHAT DO YOU BELIEVE?

Have you ever seen something in a new way and suddenly felt different towards it?

A lot of people associate success with money, yet some who have money in the bank believe they are not truly successful. Why?

There are several reasons they might believe this: they have negative associations with money and are unable to see what an increase in wealth could do for their lives and others; they don't feel worthy of the money; or they are simply not doing what brings them joy. For example, their business is giving them a decent profit but they are not having fun or enjoying life. I discuss not feeling worthy in part three and not doing what brings them joy in part two. Here in part one, I will address the associations with money and I encourage you to open up to the possibilities of what money could do for you, your family, friends, customers and others.

In this first section we look at your mindset and beliefs around money. We will look at the opinions you may have formed about money, which are intricately linked with your business success. I explain where your beliefs have come from, and ask you to explore your current held beliefs. I then ask you to consider whether this is in alignment to your business goal. There is no right or wrong belief. It is about identifying an opinion that will serve your business success. This section also explains how you make associations in alignment with these beliefs, and how that can stifle your growth. I encourage you to be a scientist, and do some tests to explore the truth in your mindset.

All of us learn how to view the world from our parents, grandparents, teachers, the media and society. This makes perfect sense because life would be quite exhausting if we had to learn everything from scratch! Imagine being born into this world and not knowing who to approach, or where to go, to learn to eat, walk, talk or write!

In science, there is a school of thought that we have certain behaviours at birth, these are called innate behaviours. No-one really knows how we know these things (although those who are spiritual have a theory) but it is currently thought they are programmed in our DNA. This is more obvious with plants, trees and animals. They just seem to know what to do. Additionally, we also learn from our environment and this has been proven in science. This is called learned behaviour.

For example, we learn how to talk from those around us. Each baby born into this world has the ability to talk any language. A baby born to English speaking parents will learn how to speak English, whilst a baby born to Chinese speaking parents will learn how to speak Chinese. They will both learn how to walk from copying the actions of those around them and later how to behave - they will get rewarded for good behaviour, and reprimanded for bad behaviour.

In summary we learn some very useful things from our guardians, teachers and environments, but, we also learn some not so good things from them too. For example Mark's parents made a few special dishes (and taught him) but generally they were not so great at cooking. So Mark believed the same of himself too. It might have been because they said everything else was too difficult for them and he believed that. From his parent's perspective every other dish was difficult. However, when Mark started to live on his own and attempted a few additional dishes to impress his partner and friends, he realised that it was not that difficult after all. He just needed to give it attention and practice, which is something his parents didn't have.

The same applies in business. Every day I hear business owners repeat the same behaviours and beliefs as their parents, predecessors/colleagues or what is written in the media. Some are useful to their growth and some are hampering their success.

Many of my clients' parents were not successful in business and some even declared bankruptcy. Sadly, some of my clients think the same will happen to them too. Naturally it's good to be cautious with money when running a business but unfortunately focusing on this fear is restricting their potential. They are kind-hearted people but they hold back in business fearing that success will make them vulnerable. Additionally, they feel that if they were to have lots of money, they will just lose it like their parents, so what's the point of trying!

I hear these same messages, and more, throughout our society. The problem is that they enter into the back door of your belief systems (via your subconscious) and you accept them to be true. I believe they are wrong, because I believe there is no such thing as failure. 'Failure' tells me that the competing drives of your mind were not aligned. Additionally, I believe that when things don't go according to how you wish them to be, you are given an opportunity to learn from the experience and make the world a better place to live.

I have come across so many amazing businesses who have the knowhow to make a positive influence in so many lives, yet they back down from making their business a success because they fear they will fail, or worse, that the money will change them into a thoughtless, uncaring, greedy person.

Does this resonate with you?

If so, I am going to share something with you.
I told one of my mentors a few years ago that I often felt like a black sheep. I didn't believe in what others said or did and this troubled me at times. It felt lonely. Avril encouraged me to BE that black sheep, in fact we decided that a purple sheep was way cooler! I gained momentum, and encouragement, to say what I thought and before long I realised lots of other people were just like me. They were often just hiding in a corner or sitting quietly in a group afraid to speak out. Through their support I was encouraged to spread my message and hence this book is now in your hands. I urge you to be who you really are too.

Explore what you currently think of money for no other reason than so you can feel more at peace and more inspired to grow your business.

I often have clients asking how can they make more money, yet they stipulate that they don't want to pay any tax. That is like asking a sports coach what you can do to get fit but also telling them you refuse to do any exercise. There are better ways of making use of money efficiently and avoid paying any unnecessary tax but thinking differently about money will change what you think of tax too. Sorry!

For example, during tax return season in the UK, clients I had been coaching for a few years felt confident to do their tax return themselves. They were pleased that they had tax to pay (as it meant their business was making a profit) and they even told me they found pleasure in doing their tax return on their own. It gave them a sense of accomplishment that they were in control of their money.

You have a choice.

You can either think of tax as something you don't like paying, or you can think of paying tax as a sign that your business is doing really well. Unfortunately, you may also be thinking you don't like what the government is doing with your money. Sorry, I cannot help you with that one other than suggesting you vote for someone else, or better still, run for election yourself! Although, I do encourage you to look at what you do get for your tax and compare this to other countries.

I want to help you so you can help your customers, follow your passion and live your purpose. In this section I will shine a light on money in a way you may never have viewed it before. I encourage you to align what you think, feel and do with money so you can have a successful business. You either want a healthy successful business or you do not. There is no right or wrong.

Top takeaway from this chapter:

We have innate behaviours as well as learned behaviours. This also applies to our beliefs. Your learned beliefs are a result of what you have absorbed from your parents, teachers, society and the media. These are neither right nor wrong, but they may be preventing you from growing your business.

WHAT DO YOU CURRENTLY THINK ABOUT MONEY?

Running a business is very similar to disciplining yourself to achieve any goal. It involves taking action but primarily it comes down to the quality of your mindset.

Many people believe that to have money they have to compromise their values and do things they are naturally unwilling to do, usually something unscrupulous and/or illegal comes to mind. This is a myth. If you want to have a successful business, you have to make changes to how you interact with money. You have to think different thoughts and take different actions, but you will always stay true to what is important to you.

What do you think about money right now?
- ✓   It is greedy to have too much.
- ✓   It gives me a sense of independence.
- ✓   It makes me feel successful.
- ✓   It is incredible useful.
- ✓   It gives me a sense of safety
- ✓   Too much money makes me feel dirty and ruthless.
- ✓   I can buy so many treats with it!

You can choose to look at money as a bad thing or a good thing. Just like you can and do with people. If you look at a photograph of a stranger standing motionless, you have no idea if they are nice or not. It is only once you start to learn about their behaviours before you can then make that judgement, but that is all it will be, a judgement.

When you meet someone new, you can choose to see their flaws or you can choose to see the good things about that person. Usually when you fall in love with someone, all you see is their good side and it is only when they annoy you, or you are thinking of leaving them, you start to list all the horrible and frustrating things about them.

Money itself is neither good nor bad. Money is like the photograph of the stranger. It is a tangible object but without a person it can do nothing! If you were to give money to a baby they would see the coins as a mixture of light and heavy metal objects, and the notes just paper. They may attempt to eat the coins or throw them like a ball. They may even rip the paper notes up into little shreds like they do with wrapping paper. They see money for what it really is. An object!

Explore how you really feel about money right now. Take some money from your pocket, or purse, and place some coins in your hand. Notice how you feel about them. Then exchange the coins for a £5, or £10 note, and again notice how you feel. If you don't have any cash, just imagine what the coins and the notes, would look like and feel like in your hand.

Now imagine you have £100 in your hand and again notice how you feel. Then imagine cash to the value of £1,000 sitting in your hand. Becoming fully aware of how you feel and what you are thinking. Then do the same for £1,000,000 and notice how you feel, and again what you are thinking.

I urge you to stay with this exercise for a while until you notice how you feel. When I do this exercise with my clients they are always surprised by their reaction. I even learnt a few things about myself when I first did a similar exercise.

What I feel, see or hear when I hold/ imagine the coins?

What I feel, see or hear when I hold/ imagine the £5/£10 note?

What I feel, see or hear when I imagine £100?

What I feel, see or hear when I imagine £1,000?

What I feel, see or hear when I imagine £1,000,000?

Is there anything else that comes to mind when I think of money?

If cash is just paper and shiny metal objects, then why does it cause so much upset, desire and/or stress?

Quite simply, it is all to do with the thoughts you are choosing to think based on past experiences and old beliefs. It is either your own past experiences with money that make you have an opinion about it, or it is the experiences of your parents, grandparents or friends, who have told you repeatedly what happened to them. What you likely thought, or were told, is that it is either something to be desired, for security, or it is something to spend because saving is being greedy!

What thoughts, feelings, or memories came up when you did this exercise? Do you know why you feel like this? Maybe the thought was said in a voice that you are familiar with, or someone you know came into your awareness. Maybe it was a memory from an experience, or maybe even the voice of a character on your favourite TV programme when younger (seriously, these characters can have such an impact on a young mind!), or a parent/grandparent.

A feeling and a thought go together although sometimes you can feel something and have no idea why you feel that way. Every millisecond a new thought comes into your mind and unconsciously you choose which one to listen to. That thought will then turn into a feeling and that's usually when most people notice it.

By doing the exercise above, it encourages you to be more mindful of how you choose to think about money. It's like tuning into a radio station and turning the volume up so you can hear it. By doing this you can then associate a feeling to a thought, just like you can associate what type of music a radio stations plays when you tune into it.

Practising mindfulness and meditation can also be beneficial if you are unaware of the thoughts that are creating your feelings about money, or with another issue. At the back of this book I have listed some great trainers. There's also a fabulous technique called generative trance that I have learned which brings together mindfulness, meditation and hypnotherapy. I share links to a couple of audios in the additional resources chapter at the end.

Generative trance is a technique that was introduced by a psychologist called Steven Gilligan who trained as a hypnotherapist under Milton Erikson, an influential figure in hypnotherapy. My trainer, Newlands Personal Development learned it from Gilligan and taught me. It brings together an understanding and compassion to our behaviour, which aligns our mind, body and spirit. This technique is the foundation of this book as it acknowledges that the individual always knows what is right for them. They sometimes just need a little guidance to create the space to find that solution.

Top takeaway from this chapter:

Money is simply paper and metal.
It is our beliefs and experiences that give it meaning.

YOUR EXPERIENCES OF MONEY

Now that you have an indication of what you think about money, I want you to consider exploring that further with a view to changing to a more helpful belief that will allow you to have a successful business. Explore why you perceive money the way you do, and that all begins with your early experiences with money.

As mentioned before, you might have modelled the behaviour of your parents, grandparents and teachers who in turn will have learnt from their parents, grandparents and teachers. You may also have collected some ideas about how to behave with money from your favourite characters on TV, or through other media channels. Remember everyone is always doing the best they can with the knowledge they have available.

Occasionally an emotional experience either when younger or later in life will have a significant influence too. If we don't learn from an opinion someone else has about money, then we learn from our experiences. I share mine and another client's situations shortly just to show the contrast of two conflicting views of money.

Personal experiences create a core belief about money for us all. If they help you to be successful in your business then they are ok, but if they are preventing you from being successful (and more on what that actually means in part two) then you can choose what you really want to believe. You can either continue buying into this core belief and settle with an unsuccessful business, or you can choose to tweak it so you can succeed.

It is always up to you. Neither myself, nor anyone else can tell you to change your beliefs. They are yours and only yours. It is up to you to explore if they help you or not and what you want to do about that.

My story: why I believe money brings me security

Money for me has always been a driver. My father was a violent alcoholic and I heard him, then later watched him, repeatedly hit my mum. My brother and I kept out the way when younger, but as we grew older we got braver and more protective over our mother. One night, when I was aged ten years old, it got pretty nasty. For the purposes of this book I don't need to go into the details but it was enough for us to run to the safety of my gran's house. It was not the first time we had done that but it was the first time we stayed there for quite a few days before going back.

I had hoped that it had been enough for mum to decide to finally leave dad but unfortunately not. I recall arguing with my mum as to why we had to go back to him. She explained to me that the money she earned from her part time jobs was not enough to feed us, clothe us and pay the bills. She relied on what little money our father did give her to top up her income. In that moment, aged ten years old, I vowed I would always have enough money and would never be dependent on anyone.

From that moment on, money meant safety, security, freedom and financial independence. Since then and until fairly recently, I had a passion for money that at times would embarrass me, but thankfully I was able to hide behind my label as an accountant.

These beliefs served me very well but often I found myself choosing to base my decisions on just money, as opposed to aligning my mind with my heart, body and soul. Therefore, I needed to tweak it, in order for me to have a successful business but more on that later.

Money from another perspective:

Other people can perceive money to be greedy and long hours away from home. One of my clients, June, associated money with hardship because her ex-husband had been keen on saving and didn't like spending any of it. They'd been in business together too and June often found herself working long hours yet not getting any reward for it.

When chatting about her associations with money June explained to me *"Money is a stealer of time. What's the point of working hard if I can't spend the money I earn?"* She went on to explain that when she divorced from her husband he used money as a *'weapon'* when it came to needing money to buy food and clothes for her children.

June associated money as the opposite of me. Where I saw freedom and safety, she saw restrictions, suffocation and control. One thing I love about coaching people on this topic is that I find there are so many different ways we all look at money.

In NLP (neuro-linguistic programming) there is a technique called perceptual positioning, which gives someone the opportunity to see their challenge from another person's point of view. This technique highlights that there are other ways to see what we see. This is something that applies to our everyday life. It can be as significant as money, or it can be as small as what we see when we first walk into a room. The important bit to remember is that there is always another point of view.

I have had some clients who have earned lots of money but they have then quickly spent it because it makes them feel bad due to associating money with greed. This is very common amongst therapists and healers. They have a kind heart and want to help everyone. This is a wonderful quality to have but the downside is that they can sometimes feel guilty when they read or hear about a world disaster that needs donations or someone closer to home is struggling, when they have money in their bank account.

Money can also affect relationships as well as our business success

Money is thought to cause upset in relationships too. The money itself is not the problem but it's the behaviour that is associated with it. For example, if someone has less income than their partner or friends, and they are embarrassed, they may not be honest about it. I once had a client come to me asking for help when his relationship with his wife broke down.

John's wife was angry when she discovered he was in debt because he'd not told her he earned less than her. She thought he'd been spending his money recklessly but when we sat down together and analysed the last twelve months' expenditure it'd all been on utility bills, grocery shopping and trips away with his wife. She had been getting annual salary increases in addition to more responsibilities, which had created stress in her life. John had thought he was doing the right thing by using his overdraft, then getting a loan, so he could take her away on long weekends to enable her to relax. Sadly, because he'd not been honest about his finances with her, their relationship broke down. Although she could understand what he did, John hadn't been honest with her, and that made her question what else he was not being honest about.

No-one is wrong or right. It is just our perception.

A lot of people either spend what money they have fairly quickly, fearful that they will lose it, or they just focus on making more of it to make them feel safe. The secret is to let go of the fear, the judgement, and all associations you have with money. Some people believe that rich people are awful people who do bad things or that money makes them nasty evil individuals. If any of these apply to you, know that it is just a belief or an association that may need to be upgraded just like an out of date computer program.

Money can also be about planning for an early retirement, travelling the world, a safety net in case anything happens, having money to buy things for the people we love or donating money to charity. What I find fascinating is that it is all about our experiences with money that make us have a certain perception of it, and that in turn will determine our relationship with it.

The underling truth is that there will always be good and bad associations with money. All I ask is that you open up to the possibility that there is another way to view your money if you are currently having negative associations with it. Remember too, whatever you believe to be true about money will differ to someone else.

You will have noticed that all the examples above are things that happen in our private lives. Yet they affect our business. Why? Quite simply because if we have a negative association with money in our personal life then this will affect money in our business. That is how beliefs and associations work.

You can be introduced to an idea one day, then see others believing that same idea. Then more events in your life appear to confirm that idea. Before you know it, that idea you were introduced to, is now a fact in your mind. It is a belief. You never question it. That is until you meet someone like me!

Top takeaway from this chapter:

Our experiences, in addition to our beliefs, shape how we see money and whether or not we associate money with something positive or something negative.

UNDERSTANDING MONEY

In order for us to make something happen in our life we need to make it conscious, give it attention and understand everything we can about it.

To enable you to have a successful business, you need to understand what money actually is, what your accounts are telling you and be conscious of your behaviour and mindset. I therefore encourage you to think about where money actually came from and why.

Money explained

A long time ago (circa 1000 BC) whenever our ancestors wanted anything they would exchange it for something that they had in their possession (e.g. rice) or within their capabilities (e.g. labour) in order to get the thing they wanted and/or needed. Then the process of bartering would take place. Someone would assess the value of the thing they wanted (e.g. shelter) and the seller would then inform the buyer of what they had to do, or give, to get that. Quite possibly some negotiations would follow depending on how much the buyer desired what they were buying or how eager the seller was to sell.

However not everyone had something another wanted or had something available to 'sell'. Labour was usually always accessible but sometimes the seller would not want what the buyer had to exchange, or it was just too tiresome travelling everywhere with what they had available to sell ie rice, livestock etc. Metals such as gold and silver were used too but not everyone had access to these resources and again these were heavy to carry around.

Therefore, circa 650-700 BC money as we now know it; was introduced. It was a while before most of the world used coins to buy and sell goods. Even now you may find that coins are still not used in some unique cultures.

In recent times, I have witnessed many businesses do a form of bartering called swaps; an exchange of their services. It works well with therapists, and I was pleasantly surprised to hear a friend who is a therapist, gets her central heating fixed in exchange for reiki sessions. I think this is pretty cool but sadly it only works if you both have something the other needs. (Try going to your local shop, or the supermarket, to get your weekly groceries in exchange for your services if you don't believe me. If you get arrested don't blame me ...)

One thing that has remained from before 1000 BC is 'value'. The exchange of goods or services has a value and this is how the price is determined. In an ideal world the price would be the same for everyone and everything but it's not. Not everyone wants the same thing and this is why it can be challenging to value another person's services or goods. If you don't want what's being sold, then any price to you will be too high.

Top takeaway from this chapter:

Money is a concept that was introduced to enable services and goods to be exchanged easier.

UNDERSTANDING BEHAVIOUR

The beliefs and judgement we hold about money are a result of an association we have all made due to experiences when younger.

To have a successful business, you need to understand your experiences and reactions a little more. I am not suggesting that you do a degree in psychology but I would suggest that you learn what you can from the background information in this book and anything else that you feel drawn to.

If you are fearful of money, or you perceive money as being ruthless and unethical, then bring to mind the experience(s) that you associate it with. *If this was a very emotional memory, then please only do this with an experienced therapist or coach. (I have a few listed in the back of this book that I would recommend but if you live further afield then please seek out someone who could help you.)*

Imagine that you are back in the experience but you are the other person (or persons) in that memory. This is not something that can be done easily but be patient and just imagine seeing the world through their eyes. Consider what was going on for them at that time. If this is difficult for you to do, just imagine that there was a positive intention behind their behaviour, or maybe it was simply the best they could offer. Maybe they didn't know what to do and panicked.

For example, this was what came up in a session I had with a client. Alice's parents' business failed when she was younger and they ended up bankrupt. Her mother implemented a course of action that Alice had always felt bitter about. During the session where we safely visualised going back to that time using a combination of NLP and hypnotherapy techniques, Alice gained insight as to why her mother possibly did what she did and why. She was also able to understand the actions that led up to the bankruptcy better, so this exercise helped Alice to gain an insight into her mother's actions, as well as addressing the fear she had towards her own business success.

The exercise was useful to Alice because she was now looking at the experience from an adult perspective as opposed to a five-year-old child's perspective. This is something that was useful for me too when I reviewed the actions of my mother when I was ten years old. I didn't understand things like debt back then, but I can now see why she did what she did and I also found out later that she also planned her financial escape that day too. She couldn't tell me though in case I let the secret out.

If a key person in the experience is still alive and you are able to talk to them without getting upset, then I encourage you to make attempts to do that. Ask them why they did what they did. Most of my clients have done this and it has brought them clarity. Often the person was unaware of behaving the way they did, or that it would have had such an impact on my client.

It reminds me of a great story that I was told during my NLP training. A young lady was cooking roast lamb in the oven by chopping the meat in two and putting it in separate trays. Her husband asked why she did it like that and she replied saying because that was the way her mum taught her. When the wife's mum came over for dinner one night, they asked her why she cooked the lamb like that. She replied, that she learnt it from her mum. Thankfully the wife's gran was still alive and when they asked her, she replied "Ach it was because my oven was small, and it couldn't take a whole lamb on one shelf".

Sometimes people do things for a reason; other times they are just copying the behaviours of others!

Top takeaway from this chapter:

If a particular experience with money bothers you, whether it was thirty years ago, or five years ago, travel back in your mind (if it is emotionally safe to do so) and look at the experience with an adult perspective, or just knowing what you know now if it was more recent.
Ask yourself what was going on for the other person, or people at that time, and what was their state of mind?
Was their mind stable and balanced or where they coming from a place of fear, stress or guilt?

WHAT DO YOU THINK ABOUT OTHER BUSINESSES?

What you think of other businesses can unlock your beliefs about money.

I overhear many business owners making comments about other businesses, including charities, being greedy and unethical, and this angers them. If you do this too, then I encourage you to gain an understanding behind the organisation that irritates you. Research as much as you can about the subject. Stay away from people's opinions, or at least ensure you see both sides (those for and those against).

Think about how difficult and challenging it can be to make decisions in your own business. Think about the mistakes you have made and how annoyed you were afterwards in hindsight about making the wrong choices. I am not saying that there are not any unscrupulous businesses but I am asking for you to consider just how challenging running a business is, especially an international one.

Many businesses and organisations have many people to please: their customers, their shareholders, their employees, politicians, and so many others. It is challenging for them to please everyone and often they are a bit lost. In fact, I believe many of them could do with an alignment of their 'head, heart, body and soul' minds. Perhaps next time you get irritated with them you should send them a copy of this book?

I truly believe they are lost and could do with some compassion. We all make mistakes. I challenge you to look back on your life, particularly your business, and ask if you have always made a decision that you still believe it was the right one now.

What decision have you regretted in hindsight? If you have none then I congratulate you, but sadly there are many business owners that have regrets. I believe therefore we should be compassionate with ourselves and others who make bad choices.

Whenever I see a person or a business doing something that I don't like I say 'Thank you for showing me what NOT to do!' I use their actions as inspiration to run my business in a way that resonates with me, as there can be times when I don't know what to do. By looking at the good and bad behaviours of others I can decide what kind of person I want to be, or not to be, and what kind of business I want to have, or not to have.

There is a saying in Scotland, where I currently live, that if you hold a piece of hot coal the only person you are hurting is yourself. If you have ever been angry you will know that every time you think of this experience, you feel pain. You believe that holding onto that anger will keep you from making the same mistake. It will, but (just like the hot coal) it will also hurt you.

If you let go and trust that you will always remember that experience, it will not hurt you anymore. The person or organisation may still continue to be part of your life but trust that one day they will learn from their mistakes. It might be in your lifetime, but it might not be, but trust that it will happen. However, even if they don't, it is far better to have a life of happiness than one of hate. It is always your choice though.

Your body is made up of cells. These cells contain atoms. Atoms are energy. You are energy. Your feelings are an indication of the energy level that you are vibrating at. Whatever level this is, is what you will attract in your life. If you are a kind and compassionate person but have a hatred of money due to experiences with an individual or an organisation, then this is what you will be attracting in your life. You will be attracting kindness and compassion but equally you will be attracting hatred and a lack of money.

If you are thinking the energy description is a bit far out there (and some days it seems a bit far-fetched for me too) then think of it like knowing what a friend does and does not like. If they complain about how horrible alcohol is all the time then you will never buy them a bottle of wine for their birthday. Although, you would likely get quite confused if you go out for dinner with them and they ask the waiter for a glass of wine.

The laws of life are no different. 'Like attracts like' so if you ask for money you will get it, but if you complain about money you will just get more reasons to complain about money, and those around you will get confused. Do you want money or do you not want money? Be passionate and clear about what you want.

Top takeaway from this chapter:

Understand that running a business, any business, is tough when it comes to making decisions. The more people a business has to please; the more people they will be unable to please.
If your head is aligned with your heart, body and soul then the decisions you make will be better aligned to your business success. Any business that is not doing this should be sent a copy of this book... ☺

OPPORTUNITY OR OBSTACLE?

The most obvious difference between a successful business and one on course to fail, is their mindset.

Successful businesses see opportunity and potential in everything. This is one of the reasons why you will see a successful entrepreneur be involved in so many business projects. Additionally, they believe anything is possible.

Looking at everything as an opportunity is one of the major differences to that of someone who achieves success and someone who works hard but never actually gets there. Life will throw things at you no matter what side of the fence you sit on. You have a choice. You can either view it as an obstacle, or as an opportunity.

If you view it as an obstacle, then I believe you will forever be in a state of depression. I certainly was! If you look at it as an opportunity, then doors will open for you. They will open for you when you see the events as obstacles too but because you are focussed on the problems you will not see the open doors. This has actually been proven in psychology experiments – we only see what we look for. There is a non-scientific technique that can help how you view things and it is quite simply, practising gratitude.

If you practise being grateful for everything that is happening in your life, then you start to see the good things that you have as opposed to the crappy stuff going on. The crappy stuff does not disappear but by changing how you look at it, it changes your outlook on life and that in turn changes how you interact with it and/or with others in your environment. It also leads to new behaviours that can help your business.

For example, a client and I were talking recently about cancellations. Any service business knows when someone cancels it can be a nuisance, particularly if you have a waiting list of people to see you. It can also mean that you don't get paid for that session. Lucy and I discussed the opportunities that she has when someone cancels. It meant she could do some research, follow up on some emails or think about her marketing. This was encouraging to her but she still had a fear of not getting paid, and as her business was barely making a profit this worried her.

After analysing her costs and time, we identified that (a) Lucy was not charging enough to cover situations like this and (b) she was not making enough money on a session even if she was fully booked. This obstacle gave her the opportunity to gain an insight into her finances and motivated Lucy to increase her price. She then also implemented a new policy where when she offered a discounted price; she made her customers pay upfront and had a no refunds policy on cancellations.

This is an example of when you need to listen to the cognitive mind. Life brings chaos and you cannot insure yourself against every eventuality but boundaries do need to be put in place. We'll talk more about boundaries in part three, but in the meantime, look at every annoying experience that happens as a reminder that something needs to change in your business.

Additionally, bigger opportunities, disguised as massive obstacles, can come along such as a change of legislation that can really change what you do and how you interact with your customers. An example would be the recent online VAT changes in the UK and other European countries that affected businesses who sell online services. At the time of writing, many are still protesting about it, and hope to see a change of policy. However, it has not stopped them from changing what they do and adapting their business services to fit within the new boundaries - it encouraged them to redefine what they offer their customers further afield. It was certainly annoying for them, but equally their actions displayed a sense of flexibility and this is what will determine a successful business to that of an unsuccessful one.

A successful business means having a flexible mindset.

We are naturally set up to adopt routines; it conserves the energy our brain uses. Remember our brain is a thirsty organ and it needs to reserve energy to be assigned to more worthwhile tasks. It therefore learns routine and shortcuts.

Yet, we are very similar to nature too, and nature likes change. As long as we are a part of nature and interacting with others, we will have to adapt to change. The best way for this to flow effortlessly is to allow it to happen, to an extent, but look for the positives. What does this allow you to do now? What would need to happen for you to adapt to this kind of experience more easily?

Top takeaway from this chapter:

To have a successful business, you are encouraged to look at your behaviours in reaction to certain experiences, asking what I am doing to resist this, and what could I do to adapt to it.

ACCOUNTABILITY OF YOUR BELIEFS

Accept responsibility for your own choice of belief.

It is important to recognise that your beliefs are not facts. They are what you perceive to be true. Everyone has different beliefs to you. You likely hang around with people who share similar beliefs to you, occasionally though, you will come across people who disagree with you. No-one is ever wrong. You just believe different things.

Consider if your beliefs are contributing to your success or hampering it. You have thought these beliefs to be true up until today and they have been incredibly useful for you to live your life and steer your business by. However, from today onwards, I want you to listen to your emotions as they guide you and let you know whether a belief is serving you well, or not.

If you feel crap, upset or angry then are you thinking something that is not serving you well? If so, it is a good indication of your heart and soul telling you it is time to change a belief. If you feel good and happy, it is a good indication that your beliefs are in alignment.

Certain emotions can be good for us up to a level. Stress and anger can often motivate and encourage us, but too much can make us mentally ill. Only you will know if you feel motivated or compressed with the emotions. Frustration can propel us into taking action, but anger on its own can move us further away from our goal.

When I am feeling a bit low, I always ask myself two questions which I will share with you.

1. What am I thinking?
2. Is this thought compassionate and understanding, or is it fearful and critical?

If I identify the thought(s) as being fearful and critical (which it usually is if I'm feeling low) then I know I have to either explore why I'm thinking that way, and/or choose a more uplifting thought.

I have listed the seven most common unhealthy beliefs/myths I have come across from other business owners which are not very encouraging for a successful business. It is good to challenge these beliefs and I give suggestions as to a better way to address them. My opinion is as much right, or wrong, as yours.

All I am asking is that you consider an alternative viewpoint and explore whether this would help or hinder as you reach for success.

Myth No 1 - rich people are bad people.

Rich people are as much bad people as any poor person is; it is the person's action that makes them appear bad, not the money. If you are an honest, kind, caring person now, then whether you have one pound, one hundred pounds, or one million pounds, you will still be an honest kind, caring person.

It is not the amount of (or lack of) money in the bank account that makes someone behave in the way they do. It is their mindset. If someone is appearing greedy it is because they don't believe they have enough money. Furthermore, someone who is stealing is doing so because they believe they don't have enough money. Both are coming from a place of fear and lack. It is their own actions, which are a result of their beliefs and experiences that make them do what they do.

I have had the pleasure of working with a few millionaires, and my gran worked for a family who owned a large successful international company. Neither my gran, nor I, have ever seen or heard any of them do anything that could be remotely considered bad. In fact, the millionaires I know are incredibly down to earth and have never forgotten their roots.

One successful multi-millionaire businessman I worked with told an audience over dinner he was still a bicycle repair man (this was the first job he ever had). Another international millionaire still makes time to see his mother on her birthday. The family my gran worked for, were incredibly thoughtful and kind. The kids she looked after still keep in touch with her by sending letters. Their mother, the lady my gran worked for, pops round to see her a few times a year to say hi, and catch up on what's been happening. In fact, my gran was recently in hospital and she got a visit from this lady.

Neither the kids, nor my gran's ex-employer, have a duty to keep in contact with my gran (she stopped working for them over forty years ago and they have all moved away from the village) yet they do. Why? Because they are good people. On the other hand, I have met a few 'bad' people but they have not been rich, in fact they have been quite poor. They have acted that way because they have been coming from a place of anger and feeling unloved.

Myth No 2 - Money does not bring happiness.

This belief is very dependent on your definition of happiness, however let us look more closely at it; money brings or does not bring something. Remember money is just a concept, a thing that was brought into existence to make the buying and selling of goods and services easier to manage. It is not the money itself that brings about happiness or unhappiness, it is what you do with the money, and what experiences you recall, that determine whether or not it brings you happiness.

In my first eBook *12 Steps to Improve Your Cashflow* I gave the example of buying a holiday with money. Money can buy you a holiday but your own actions will determine whether you enjoy the holiday or not, hence whether it gives you happiness or not. This goes for everything. What you do with it, and how you respond to anything in your life will determine your happiness. Life will throw things at you for a variety of reasons, but you always have a choice what to think, feel and do in all situations. If you disagree with me, I highly recommend that you read about a book called *'Breakthrough: A blueprint for your mind'* by Brian Costello, or any other NLP and psychology books you have to hand.

Myth No 3 – My accounts keep reminding me that I don't have enough money so why bother looking at them.

It is a common reaction to ignore something because you fear what the information is telling you. However, this is the worst thing you can do because by not keeping an eye on what you are spending you could lose a lot more money. Denial is a common response to a fear, and it's one of the most common defensive mechanisms our brain adopts. There are loads and it's all quite fascinating, which is why we must be compassionate with our actions, even those at an unconscious level.

People can adopt defensive mechanisms for a number of reasons. For instance, guilt through fear of judgement, or unease about appearing greedy. That guilt then kick-starts feelings of stress and anger that spiral out of control and negatively influence decision making. Strangely there is a part of us, one of the competing minds (head, heart, body, or soul), that thinks this is a good idea. Each of your minds are just trying to protect you and do what is best for you. Unfortunately, they just all have different strategies on how to do that...

The way to stop yourself adopting a defence mechanism or at least to reduce the number of times you do so, is to understand the rationale behind your behaviour and above all, go easy on yourself. There is always a positive intention behind any behaviour. Always. You just have to ask what is it that I am protecting? What is it that I am not doing and why?

Find a good friendly accountant (yes there are some), or a finance coach. Choose someone you can relax easily with, and get them to help you pull together a cashflow forecast and discuss your expenditure on a regular basis. This will make it easier to approach. I offer a free cashflow template in week four if you sign up to the free implementation support that coincides with my eBook *12 steps to improve your cashflow*. You can get a copy by registering here:

www.hmcoaching.co.uk/ebook-cashflow

Remember I told you earlier about Alice, who got a better insight into her mum's behaviour around her father's bankruptcy? She had a fear of accounts because she didn't want to be presented with information that told her that the business was not going very well. This was because of her father's bankruptcy and therefore she didn't want to face such a traumatic event again. Yet she could see that what she was doing was not helping, so she went through the motions of looking at her accounts. It was not until she understood her mother's behaviour better that she could look at her accounts with renewed energy. Then when she was able to bring compassion into her behaviour and of those around her without judgement, she was finally able to move forward. This is also the action that I had to adopt too which is why I can recognise it in others.

I can completely resonate with you not wanting to be reminded of how little you have but know that if you get that information quickly you have an opportunity to change what is not working and therefore prevent any failure. I went through a period of denial, which as an accountant I am not proud of, yet I want to share it with you to help you recognise that we all have defence mechanisms even with the best of intentions. I expand on this in part four where I tell you why and what I had to do to overcome it. In the meantime, trust that it may be tough now, but it will be tougher the longer you leave it. I have a couple of friends who experienced bankruptcy who will happily answer any questions you have, if you ever want to know just how tough it can get!

Myth No 4 - I'm not a logical, detailed person so I don't like doing my book-keeping.

There is a false belief that your accounts should be set out in a certain way. If you are a limited company your accounts should be in the required format for the authorities but your accountant can do all that. Your day to day accounts, however, can be in any system that works for you. This can be a notebook, ticking off your bank statement, a spreadsheet, or an accounts software package. It can be updated daily, weekly, fortnightly or monthly. The numbers can be horizontal or vertical and the categories can be whatever groups make sense to you.

It is crucial that the system you use fits in with the kind of person you are. For example, someone who is very logical will have a completely different system to someone who is creative. There are loads of accounts workshops available but it is important that you don't feel you have to stick to the given template, otherwise you will be trying to fit a square peg into a round hole. Choose what works for you, and if you need help or just want to check your system is ok, ask your accountant or a finance coach to check it over and give you feedback. However, as long as your system identifies all your expenditure and income easily, it is updated regularly and highlights key performance measures, then it is perfect!

Myth No. 5 - I don't like accountants.

Sadly, a small minority of business owners have had a bad experience with accountants which leaves them thinking all accountants are like that. Every business/individual is different. It is crucial that you shop around for an accountant that you can trust and relax with. Ask around for recommendations, but also remember that your friend's accountant might not be the best one for you.

I have been working with a client for over a year now who had previously worked with another accountant until finding me. He recently told me *"I feel very energised and positive doing my accounts with you and have never felt that when doing my accounts before."* Trust that the right accountant is out there for you. Meet them over a cup of coffee or spend a little time chatting to them on the phone. Do not be afraid to ask questions or ask them to explain something until you understand it. I always offer a free initial consultation call and most accountants I know do this too.

Myth No 6 - I cannot understand my accounts.

Accounts are just a story but written in numbers instead of words. It's a bit like learning a new language. For example, when you first learnt a foreign language in school, it is likely that none of it made sense but gradually with a good teacher, lots of books and audios, you learnt how to order your dinner when you go on holiday.

All it takes is patience and a good teacher. Find a finance coach that will teach you by explaining your accounts to you and helping you to understand how everything all comes together. You don't need to know it all at once if you don't want to. Ask then to have it explained in small bite size portions and gradually you will know everything you need to know.

Myth No 7 – The tax authorities are out to get me!

The truth is that the tax authorities want to help you. Honest! They only want to catch businesses who are deliberately manipulating their tax return. If you are running your business honestly then you have nothing to worry about!

Many clients of mine are fearful that they do something wrong and get into trouble with the tax authorities. To be honest, the formal written letters really don't help. The best way to challenge this belief is to sit down with your accountant and go through a few of their letters. You will soon see that they are really just very informative letters written in very formal English.

One client shared with me that he noticed he got panicky every time the tax authorities sent him a letter. He sat in meditation one day and explored his feelings around this. He recalled that he had received a bad exam result one year at school, and it arrived in a brown envelope similar to the colour the UK tax authorities use! He also had a fear of formal letters for this very reason too (sometimes our experiences can effect more than one thing) and he addresses this fear now by using some techniques he knows to calm himself down when he gets one. Mainly, slow deep breaths and mindfulness.

Top takeaway from this chapter:

Take ownership of your beliefs. Challenge them if they hinder you. Experiment and search out an alternative point of view; one that will help you and your business.

THE MONEY MINDSET

*The difference between those that have money and those that don't
is how they think and behave around money.*

The most common myth is that successful businesses are obsessed with profits ie money. That may be true on one level but let's explore the foundations of a successful business. A successful business, at its core, is a business that is able to reach as many people as possible with its services and products. In order for that business to be successful, it needs to make a profit; otherwise it will be unable to reach all those it potentially could. For a business to make a profit it needs to develop what I call the money mindset. I will talk about profits in more detail shortly, but I would like you to first consider the idea of 'obsession' versus 'love'.

Obsession is when you think about something constantly and have no regard to anything, or anyone, else in your environment. Obsession is often mistaken for love but these are two very different things. Loving money does not mean a business is obsessed with it, which is what the majority of unsuccessful businesses believe. In order for you to understand this further, think back to when you first fell in love.

Your first experience of love was likely aged between ten and thirteen years old and you thought about that person all the time. You probably wrote their name on all your school books, day dreamed about them and the only thing you talked about was them. Depending on your hormones, you may have even followed them around school at playtime. That was a light form of obsession.

Now think about what you did when you fell in love with your current partner, or you became aware of how much you cared about someone. You likely thought about them a lot, but not all the time, possibly because there is so much other stuff to think about! You likely didn't write their name on everything you owned, and hopefully you didn't follow them about everywhere... This was a light form of love.

You also know that this love grows into something far more incredible and powerful when you start to respect that person for who they are, and what they believe. You don't change them into someone else. You don't say horrible things about them. You give them unconditional love, you receive unconditional from them, and the love continues to deepen.

Those businesses that love money, they love it like you would your partner. They respect what it represents and they honour its value. I will talk more about value later, but for now perhaps consider that this love of money is not an obsession.

It is a respect for its existence, and what it gives them. Successful businesses think about the experiences they share with money ie being able to reach so many customers, and they most certainly don't think about money all the time, but they are aware of their finances.

Some businesses will take action on what others would associate as risky. They take risks because they need to stay true to what they are about. If they believe strongly in something, then they have to do whatever it takes to get their message or product out. They got to where they are now by grabbing opportunities and going outside their comfort zone regularly, and they just keep doing it. It is a way of life for them. They believe that, one way or another, things will always be ok, as long as they stay true to what they believe in. More often than not they just don't think about it. They only think about getting their products and services out to people.

In contrast, those businesses that don't have money, or have very little, constantly think, and worry about money. Understandably businesses that have very little cash reserves worry about losing what they already have. They worry about how long their current savings will last them. They concern themselves with just how little they do have and how that restricts them, and they lose sight of what they are supposed to be aiming for. This is how they get lost.

I am not advocating you take risks if you have no savings but the secret is getting the balance right. This is when you need to hold a meeting with your head, heart, body, and soul asking – *How can I reach more customers with the resources I have available?*

Let me just clarify something else which is quite important. Not worrying about money does not mean that you should not pay attention to your finances. It means the complete opposite. Successful businesses may have an attitude of not worrying about their money, but they do still pay attention to their finances. Not worrying, means simply not *worrying* NOT that they adopt a defence mechanism and go into denial.

Use your finances as a feedback mechanism to tell you what is working, and what is not working. Also your finances can tell you what area of your business needs attention. It means taking action. It does not mean denial.

Does it really matter who helps who?

Additionally, those businesses that are successful appreciate how profits can benefit their businesses. They relish in what a successful business can do for so many people. They want other businesses to enjoy that success too. They want their business to be successful as much as possible, and as soon as possible. If they have a product and/or service that can help people, then they want those people to know about it now! They want to keep growing their business until everyone knows about it. They also appreciate that other businesses think and feel that same way, even their competition.

Unsuccessful businesses blame their lack of growth on money and/or on their competition, who have more money, or success, than them. They fail to see that they are using the lack of money as an excuse, and not a driver. Those who have a negative mindset about money and success, will often criticise their competitors, and other businesses or organisations, who are successful in a similar area. I encourage my clients to look at their competitors as just doing the same thing that they are doing – helping people.

As long as you are working in accordance with your values and ethics, you will work with people who resonate with you. Everyone is different, which means that you will not be everyone's choice of beverage, nor will they be yours! This is where 'competitors' can be useful. You can pass people their way and they pass people your way. Better still, you could team up with them and offer so many other services and products to your customers, and everyone wins.

To get more of something, you have to give it. If you only want to be surrounded by kind people, then you need to be kind. If you want more money to invest into your business, you need invest in something that will grow your business. That can be technology, materials, labour or your own personal growth.

If you have no savings available, then you do need to rise to the challenge another way. That involves taking a risk and venturing outside your comfort zone. If you need more money to buy something, then you need to find ways of achieving that.

Top takeaway from this chapter:

Respect money for what it can do for your business. Love it, but do not become obsessed by it, nor do not fear it in abundance or lack. Venture out your comfort zone.

YOUR RELATIONSHIP WITH MONEY

In my eBook *12 Steps to Improve Your Cashflow* I introduce the concept of catching up with our finances as being the same as catching up with a friend.

I now encourage you, as I do with all my clients, to look at money as a relationship. Money, for most cultures, will always be a part of your life and like anything else, is far more pleasant if you have a good connection with it. When you run a business it is crucial, that you have a good relationship with money.

Your finance relationship in your business

Over the last twenty years I have worked with many businesses. They have differed in size, industry, culture, personality of top management and amount of money in the bank. The one thing that remained the same in terms of determining their success or failure was their mindset around their finances. Those that were successful had a good relationship with their finances, and a positive opinion of money. Those that got by, or worse failed, had a poor relationship with their finances and a negative opinion of money.

Your relationship with your finances and money is like any other relationship in your life. You will find that by improving your association with your finances and money, it will have a positive knock on effect to your other relationships. It certainly has with my clients. In fact, after challenging a client to look at money differently to how she was currently perceiving it based on past experience, she found herself in a relationship for the first time in six years!

I believe it is a myth that money ruins relationships. It is the mindset about money that causes the relationship to breakdown. I have heard many arguments and seen relationships break down as a result of spending too much, worrying about where income will come from, or the hatred they have towards those that have money. I have yet to hear of a relationship that has broken down as a result of both partners having a positive mindset around money.

Your relationship with your finances and money needs regular attention and needs a positive frame of mind. As I introduced in *12 steps to improve your cashflow*, your finances need regular catch ups to see how they are doing and what stories they have to tell this week. The longer you leave it until you next meet up with a friend the more you have to catch up on and the more time you need to hear all their news. Your finances are no different. As I was writing this book a friend of mine posted a picture online of her desk piled high with a year's receipts! Even I could sense a feeling of dread at the thought of taking on such a massive task.

Like any meeting you have with a friend or family member, it is also much more fun and uplifting when you feel positive and motivated to catch up. How often have you looked forward to meeting a friend when you know they have some exciting things going on in their life, and really paid attention to what they had to say?

Equally, how often have you ever felt deflated about meeting up with someone, and not given your full attention with them? Maybe even at the back of your mind you are asking how soon you can leave without it appearing too obvious you really didn't want to be there!

If your finances were a person what kind of relationship would you have with them?

Would you look forward to your meet ups and pay attention to their news, or would you drag yourself along half-heartedly because you feel there is a duty. Are you inspired by the news they have to tell you and walk away motivated to do something to help them, or do you run away as fast as you can and immediately do something to forget about the whole experience?

Additionally, throughout a relationship there are times when you might be asked to do things that you would not normally do. For example, go out of your way to get something to cheer them up or take them to the ballet on a special occasion when you would rather be watching a film. Your finances are no different. When you review your finances they often tell you to do something you would rather not do.

For example, when you review your finances and acknowledge that you have less income that you need and/or have too many expenses, you could either cut back on a few luxury expenses or look at different ways to get sales. Most business owners I know would rather have sales come to them effortlessly than cut back on certain expenditure (including myself!). However, your business finances will ask you to do things that get you in front of your ideal customer – but these might be things that if you had a choice, you would not want to do. This could be networking, or public speaking.

If this is you, then I encourage you to connect in with your *WHY* - your reason for doing what you do (see more on this in part two), and explore how you can help your customers. Selling is not about making money. It is about helping others. Your business exists for a reason. I can only imagine that you started your business in order to help others and/or yourself. Be specific about what you want your business to achieve. How do you plan on helping others? How do you intend on making your life and your family life easier and more enjoyable?

I am the type of person that likes small groups or better still, one on one relationships. I'm human too and fear criticism. I do know though, that my business is asking me to step up and do public speaking - starting with the launch of this book. I am a little nervous about this yet I know it is just a fear and that fear is just a perception. I talk more about this in part four and I will be adopting the techniques that I share with you throughout this book because I know they work.

I also discussed in *12 Steps to Improve Your Cashflow* how your expenses combined with your actions, can tell you a little about yourself. If you spend money on advertising, you need to ask if you are doing everything you can to get in front of those who will see your advert. Or perhaps you are disappointed with networking events because you are expecting the event to result in you walking away with a few sales?

Are you being creative in response to what you are experiencing?

Ultimately your relationship with your finances can be broken down into how much you want your business to be successful and what your opinion of money is. Success does not have to be about having lots of money in the bank account. I will cover this is in more detail in part two.

I believe success is about your business reaching as many people as it can to help them in whatever way you have chosen, and that you are happy with what you are doing. We need money to pay for technology, materials or travel in order for this happen. Therefore, for your business to be successful it needs to make a profit in order to survive and grow. For that to happen we need to have the *Money Mind*; a positive healthy relationship with our finances.

When you are inspired to review your finances regularly, and your mind is free from any negativity surrounding money, your business will be happier. You will be happier and you will find that things are much more effortless. You will feel like you are on track in achieving your business goals because you will feel like you really are doing what you set out to do. You will still have to rise to the challenge of growing your business but your mindset will be empowering and you will be inspired to look for the support you need.

Time to explore your relationship with your finances

Do you?

- Always find yourself cutting back on expenses or dipping into any savings until you get paid?
- Have irregular income?
- Wake up in a sweat in the middle of the month wondering how you are going to pay the bills next month?
- Put off doing your tax return because you don't want to know how much money you need to find to pay another bill?
- Find it difficult to price your services or products?

If you answered yes to any of the above questions, then your relationship is not as good as it could be. I know that you have likely tried various methods of solving this. You may have repeated affirmations and tried techniques such as EFT (emotional freedom technique). You may even have read some books on managing your money, or asked a fellow business owner, or maybe your coach, how they manage their money.

If you have not already done so, please do the exercises in chapter two (What do you currently think about money?) to gain an insight into what you think about your finances. There are many different reasons why none of what you tried has worked, or maybe it has worked a little but still you feel there could be improvements. Give your attention to your money because it is like any other relationship in your life. It craves attention and when it is denied the relationship breaks down. It throws a tantrum or goes in a huff. Weird as it sounds, it really is that simple.

I have had clients who are incredibly wealthy enlist me for my services to help them keep better track of their income and expenses because they do have a good relationship with their finances. They want to make it better. However, the majority of clients I have worked with have had financial challenges, and their money relationship has been non-existent. If you are one of the latter, know that you are not alone but believe that there is another way. I would not be coaching clients or have written this book otherwise!

I have found that the people behind a business will not have a loving relationship with money when they lack a truly loving relationship with themselves and those around them.

I discuss self-love in part three, when I ask if you really believe you deserve a successful business. By not loving yourself or believing you are worthy, you are not helping others get access to your services and products. It is like the air host(ess) telling you that you have a better chance of helping others, if you put on your own oxygen mask before you help children or the elderly. By loving yourself and your business first, you can really help others. If you do not, then you will run out of air.

One of the limiting beliefs many people have, in my opinion, is thinking that if you have a desire for money you are disconnecting from your heart and soul. Hopefully you now know that is not true. It is about what the person does with their money.

If someone feels insecure then yes money will likely be a passion that drives all decisions. However, if someone feels secure, feels loved, then they will have a healthy relationship with money. You can receive that security and love from others but when you do it is always dependent on them. You need to feel that within yourself.

Top takeaway from this chapter:

The stability of your relationship with your finances and what you think and feel about money will ultimately determine the success or failure of your business.

THE CHALLENGES TO PRICING AND ULTIMATELY PROFIT

When it comes to pricing, and determining a profit, it involves two stages. Most unsuccessful businesses fall at the second hurdle. When a business calculates its price, it must look at all its costs then add a little extra (accountants call this a mark-up) to cover a profit however, the business owner has to be ok with charging this price. This is where there is clear definition between a successful business and an unsuccessful business. How much do your services or products cost and what you believe them to be worth? You must then seek those who value your product/services the same way you do.

What can economics and fashion tell you about pricing and value?

Fashion is a good example of how value is determined. If you value the practicality of a jacket then you will quite happily pay a decent amount for something that will keep you warm and dry. If you are into fashion however you may be more inclined to give a higher value to the jacket that is 'this season' and a low value to the jacket that was in fashion last year or one that is plain but keeps you dry and warm. You will put a higher value on the jacket that gives you what you are looking for.

Value is always a personal preference. This was something that I discovered quite early on in my business. I had someone complain about my prices, yet I heard they went to an expensive restaurant and paid double my price for a five course meal just a few days later. This is why the cost of the product/service should always be assessed and charged at a profit then you find the customer that will value what you have to offer. Don't be put off by those who don't value your services or products. Don't discount for people who don't value what you do and NEVER sell at a loss. If this is something you struggle with then you will enjoy part three.

What do you value most?

What would you invest in?
- ✓ Training?
- ✓ More time with your family/ friends?
- ✓ Taking steps towards that dream you have always had?
- ✓ Reaching people all over the world and making a difference to their lives?

Over the years I have invested a lot of money into further education and training as learning and developing my skills is a high priority for me. In 2014 I realised the one thing I truly cared about was writing and publishing books, which was a dream I had since I was a child. I eventually sourced a team of people in 2015 to help me align my books to my business. When I mentioned the total cost to a friend, she thought it was very expensive. My friend didn't value writing a book (or helping people through that book) in the same way I did. I knew in my heart I had to do it. I am glad I did because the feeling I got when I published my first eBook; *12 Steps to Improve Your Cashflow* was amazing. I know I will be ecstatic when I have the printed version of this book! That feeling far outweighs the price in my mind.

How do I or my customers assess value/ price?

We assess the value of anything by asking ourselves five questions, usually subconsciously as we are not always aware of this. It is good to be familiar with this step from a conscious level though to assess your own expenses but also as this is what your customer is doing when it comes to your services and products.

The questions are:
1. How much do I want it?
2. Why do I really want it?
3. What feeling does it give me?
4. Is there anything else, cheaper or more accessible, that I can get right now, that will do the same job?
5. How does this price compare to something else I value?

When answering question one, it helps to think about what would happen, or how would you feel, if you didn't get this particular thing. Be aware of what you really want in your heart and soul, not just what your head says. It is important to note that if you have to get yourself into debt to buy this item then I would recommend you give a lot of attention to this decision. The second and third questions will help with question one too.

For example, my heart, body and soul said write a book. My head was saying there is no money to be made in books. My cognitive mind was outvoted yet it still needed convincing it was the right thing to do, otherwise it would have sabotaged the experience. So the meeting of my minds decided my cognitive mind was to be in charge of working out a budget so I could afford to publish a book. All the 'minds' were happy with that outcome which then allowed the action to be taken more easily.

The answer to question two and three, can be very interesting! I often find people will buy something because they think they should be buying it. This is usually either due to peer pressure ('all my friends have one', or 'everyone is doing it') or the marketing power of the branding of that particular product.

For example, most technology products can have a very powerful brand which signifies that having that particular product is like being part of a unique family. They give their customers an identity. Not having that product when all your friends do can feel like being an outsider.

I find people try to avoid question four, especially if they want it badly. This is also why people will buy something only to either return it at a later date or feel guilty about it the next day. Often those guilty feelings are masked by something else, maybe a subject for a whole other book, however I do introduce the concept of self-love in part three.

For example, when my first mentor quoted her price to me, I was taken aback. However, I then listed everything I would get from her and how much I wanted change in my life. Her price also helped me to value her time as well as my own. In hindsight what she gave me was priceless.

For the fifth question, when you compare it to something you already value you are able to appreciate what it is you are getting. Very often a price is thought to be expensive. This is usually when the person does not value the benefits of a service/product or they have very little money. When they compare it with something else they value, it helps put it in a different perspective.

For example, a fellow accountant once told me that he paid £7,000 for coaching sessions with a high profile coach who was very effective at getting results. Even I was a tad shocked at the price tag. However, he explained to me that before he signed up to the sessions, he was heavily overweight, drinking one bottle of wine every night and smoking 40 cigarettes a day. To sum it up, he was pretty unhappy with his life. The only thing he did have going for him was the savings to pay for his coach. He was desperate for change and was willing to pay for that change to get the most desired results and fast. He actually got far more than what he desired.

In four years he would have spent circa £22,000 on his addictions so he saved £15,000 PLUS he is much healthier and slimmer. That in itself is added value. Furthermore, he is now happily married and has two children. What price does he put on his health, his lovely wife and his two adorable kids? I bet it is more than £7,000!

Top takeaway from this chapter:

Price is calculated first on cost and then value. What you value will be seen in your expenditure. What your customers' value will be seen in your sales. If your customers do not see the value, do NOT discount. Check that your costs are reasonable then look for those who do see the value.

Only when you have sufficient profits can you afford to give discounts or freebies to those who are unable to afford what you have to offer.

WHY WE NEED OUR BUSINESS TO MAKE A PROFIT

"Without profit, the products and services couldn't be provided, nor could workers be kept in employment. Profit to a business is like food to a human body: the body must grow and develop – with the assistance of food; take away the supply of food and the body wastes away and eventually dies."
WCF Hartley, An Introduction to Business Accounting for Managers, 2nd edition, 1970

The biggest behavioural change that you need to make (if you are not already doing so) is to make a profit.

The advantage of being an accountant is that I get to see how much things cost. I am regularly in the company of others who complain about the price of something where I have had the privilege of either seeing how much that exact thing costs or something similar, and I know it is a bargain. I am sometimes tempted to buy the product; then tell the person they should think about increasing their prices! I always tell them upfront if I have the opportunity though.

You will know, by now, that the reason the price is low is either because that person is undervaluing their services/products due to their associations with money, or they have not fully grasped the costs against their time. The complaints from others may be because that person is attracting the energy of people who are not valuing themselves either.

There are many things that need to be taken into consideration for the price and often it is not something people think about until they have to make those products or services. As mentioned in the previous chapter, the sale price must take into account the cost of the product/service being sold to the customer, in addition to other costs that the business has. You will likely be familiar with the following exercise if you make and sell a product and if you aren't then I suggest you get familiar with it now.

Let's take a loaf of bread from the local bakery. The cost of that bread includes the ingredients such as flour, water, yeast and salt. Then there is the energy cost to run the ovens, the labour cost of the baker's time who kneaded it and baked it, a proportion of the energy cost of the kitchen/shop and labour cost of other staff members. Then there are the other costs of the shop that need to be taken into consideration; cleaning the place every day, equipment needed to bake the bread and operate the shop. In addition, there are the small things that get taken for granted, such as packaging. Then there are all the background costs that also need to be apportioned amongst the goods the baker sells likes stationery, insurance cover and other professional fees.

Apologies if you now never look at a loaf of bread in the same way again!

A profit ensures survival

I have noticed a common belief amongst some kind hearted businesses; that if you are compassionate you should not make money over and above your costs. That is not true. If you do not make any money you cannot pay your rent/mortgage and you cannot put food on the table. You cannot clothe yourself and your family or go on holiday. Is this the life you want?

A service or product should be provided as economically and efficiently as possible with the resources available so as to reach as many people as possible who need it. A business that makes a profit, or a non-profit organisation, that is reaching its users, is certainly fulfilling this requirement but by ensuring you are making a profit, it can be increased so you can reach far more people. Just think, by making a decent profit you can do other stuff to reach so many other people.

I have a client who is a community interest company currently looking at costs for a very sophisticated software to reach out and help others. They are not in business to make money but they do need to find £50,000 to pay for developing the software!

Streamlining your processes to ensure your systems and time are productive and efficient as possible, are both effective ways of getting more output from the business resources available to you (time, equipment and money). If your business generates an increase in profits though, this allows you to reinvest the money back into the business.

For example, these can be in the form of:
- Purchasing new equipment.
- Recruiting an assistant to help you.
- Funding a marketing strategy to increase awareness.
- Paying for further training and development.
- Supporting the community by donating to charity.
- Rewarding others who have supported you and recommended you.
- Giving freebies or discounted services/products to those who cannot afford your full service.

Now let's talk Cash

It is a common mistake to think our business is performing well because we have money in the bank account. We have to remember that lots of cash does not necessarily mean profit, and a profitable business does not always mean a surplus of cash. Don't fall into the trap of thinking one equals the other. Ensure you have cash in the bank AND you have a profitable business. To ensure you always have cash in the bank, it is crucial you have savings.

You can have a surplus of cash but possibly making a loss if:
- You have received income for future sales.
- Your customers are paying cash but you are getting credit from suppliers so you have not paid all your bills yet.
- You have charged VAT on your sales but you have not yet passed it on to the tax authorities.

- You are missing invoices. Some suppliers can be late in getting their invoices to you or they forget then all of a sudden you are faced with a hefty invoice. (I know of one supplier that failed to invoice a customer for almost six months!)
- You have received a grant or an investment to grow your business and not yet spent it on the resources you need.
- You have forgotten to forward on the payroll tax that has been deducted from your staff wages to the tax authorities.
- You have not yet paid your own tax bill.

You can have a profitable business but a lack of cash if:
- You are giving your customers credit but your suppliers are not giving you any credit.
- Your customers are not paying their bills on time, or at all.
- You have to buy large volumes of stock to enable you to get the best price.
- You have not invoiced your customers. You may have included the sale in the accounts but you forgot to send the invoice and it is still sitting in your bag or car glove box.

Have you got a rainy day fund?

The phrase 'money makes the world go round' may or may not be true, but it certainly helps tremendously in business. Cash is a scarce resource in most businesses and although giving your customers what they want is one element of a successful business, balancing the cashflow is another.

So how can we balance the cashflow?

Well, it is all about weighing up what comes in with what goes out and adding a little extra for reinvesting. Simple really, but it can be a challenge in reality. Especially when you are buying an asset, or incurring a marketing expense, that will not give you immediate results. Additionally, you could be buying a large volume of stock to enable you to sell to your customers in a timely manner. This is why it is important to have additional money kept aside for such purchases.

I was talking to a client recently on how he was having cashflow problems because his invoices were not being paid on time and he had a big corporation tax bill to pay. I enquired as to whether he had considered putting money aside. He laughed and said *"Yes that would have been a good thing to do. If only I did."*

You see, everyone knows they need to keep money aside, including you, but it is tempting to spend it when you have it. You do have to be disciplined with your money when running a business because you just never know when you need that rainy day fund.

If you don't already do so, start building savings that can be put aside for future investments, and for times when trade is slow ie what I call a 'rainy day'. For example, if your products or services are seasonal or you have to close the business to go on holiday, you will need money to keep you going and pay the bills throughout that period. You should always put aside money for VAT and tax too.

Build your business growth slowly where possible; have small stock reserves and never buy too many assets. Buy only the essentials that you require to trade. For example, do you really need an office, or can you work from home? Could you just rent a meeting space or hold your meetings in a quiet café just now? Do you really need the designer desk or a new van or is there a cheaper alternative?

In the UK, HMRC currently does not ask for any tax payments until the following 31st January after you set up in business as a sole-trader. For some business this can be almost twenty-one months after they first started trading. They also ask you to pay 50% towards next year's bill too. If you have traded well and not been keeping some money aside, you can be in for a massive shock!

Putting a little aside every month into savings will keep you informed of how well your business is doing. Although, if you have had a good few months but now sales have fallen or you need some money for buying equipment I would then ask your accountant to help do a draft tax return to see if you have maybe put too much aside. I certainly get asked this question a lot, especially when someone running a private limited company wants to know if they can pay themselves a dividend.

If you still experience a shortage of cash, then it is time to analyse all your expenditure. Everything that you pay out should be questioned.

- Can you get a cheaper alternative?
- Can you do it yourself?
- Could you possibly do without it for a few days/weeks/months?
- Are you getting quotes prior to work being carried out, or are you always getting a shock when the bill comes in?
- Can you reduce the credit terms you give your customers?

Ensure that all debts are collected within the period you agreed with your customer. If anyone is constantly paying late then perhaps a different arrangement should be discussed. Or if you are in the situation where you give your customers credit but you have to pay your suppliers up front, then you could either ask your suppliers to give you credit or ask your customers to pay on delivery and/or a deposit up front.

It is also important to have your products and services priced at the optimum level where both the business is making a profit and the customers still feel like they are getting value for their money. To have a successful business, means trading well and having money in the bank as well as following your heart and looking after yourself.

I have tried to keep this section light and filled with lots of ideas but I have hopefully inspired you to build a savings fund, perhaps even generated a curiosity to see if you can save some money on your expenditure, or agree better repayment terms with suppliers and customers.

Top takeaway from this chapter:

Profit is the same to our business, as food and water is to our body. Without it would get weak and eventually die. Cash in the bank is a good indication of profit but only after tax and all other bills have been accounted for.

LISTEN TO YOUR THOUGHTS/QUESTION YOUR BELIEFS

Your reality will take into account ALL of your thoughts.

I want to emphasise that if on any level you think money is greedy, or success isn't possible for you, then it will NOT happen despite your intention of helping others. I know someone who is full of love for life yet despises anyone or thing that is related to money. It is no surprise that she has a lack of money, and her business is having trouble financially.

It helps if you focus on the ideal customer and have a sense of your values when running a business and I truly encourage you to let go of judgement about money and success, in order to achieve your goals.

If you have any conflicting beliefs, then this sends out a conflicted message through your behaviour. Conflicting beliefs are quite simply beliefs that are in contrast with one another.

An example would be you running a business to have flexibility to spend time with your kids, yet believing that you must give up your weekends, evenings and time with your kids in order for your business to be successful. I talk about this is part two. Another would be asking for money for your services/products yet equally believing that asking for money is being greedy.

These are both common thoughts about money and success. It's like someone saying they want to lose weight yet hating anyone who has successfully slimmed down! I am sure you are familiar with at least someone who has yoyo dieted, muttering 'skinny bitch' under her breath at an acquaintance who has successfully downsized!

If you really think having too much money is greedy I ask you to question that belief and consider what your definition of greed is.

According to the Collins English dictionary it means *'Intense, selfish desire for wealth, power or food'.* I assume you eat, so does going to the shops and buying food make you greedy? No, because you have got to eat.

Your business needs money just as much as you need to eat. Asking for money will not make you greedy. You may have seen others behaving in a greedy manner when it comes to cash and have assumed their behaviour is linked to their desire for money. However, watching someone else buy lots of food to store in their cupboards or eat more than their body can handle does not make you do the same, does it?

Behaviour comes back to the person not the object. Money itself does not make anyone greedy. It is the person's behaviour that makes them appear greedy. Therefore, if you think having money will make you greedy, I wonder what in your personality assumes that you will adopt that behaviour. Have you been greedy before? Have you had an intense desire for money?

I think some people have, especially anyone who comes from a deprived childhood where money was scarce. They may have had an intense desire for money and then been ashamed of their behaviour. This is a natural reaction if they have been restricted financially in any way. They would have been looking after themselves in the best way they knew how. It doesn't make them a bad person. If anything, they could probably do with a bit of slack. It's as much the same as someone who has experienced a lack of love when younger, they desire love more than the average person. They crave it and base all their decision on whether or not someone will love them more as a result of their action. The same applies to anyone who craves money. This is why we need to have a meeting with our minds and have our head, heart, body and soul all in alignment.

As I mentioned in chapter three (Our experience of money), I have experienced the physical and emotional restrictions that a lack of money can bring when I was younger and my clients have shared their frustrations with me too. The experience of a lack has a significant influence in what happens afterwards, because of the beliefs attached to those experiences. These beliefs then influence your thoughts.

This happens with any experience. Your beliefs will influence your thoughts. Your thoughts will influence your feelings. If you are feeling a bit low then the chances are that you are thinking slightly negatively, unless you are unwell and your body is telling you to stop, rest and look after yourself. When you think negative, disempowering thoughts, you will feel crappy.

Additionally, your brain has a mirror signal which will mimic what it is surrounded with. Think back to whenever a fellow business owner was excited about something in their life. How did that make you feel?

Think also to a time when you were with a business owner who was moaning about something and dismissed any suggestion you gave them. How did that feel and was this feeling different to when you were with the excited person?

The chances are that when you were with the excited person you came away encouraged, excited and wanted to help them so you too could get in on the fun they were having. I am sure you wanted to help the person who was moaning too, but the chances are the next day you likely felt just as depressed as them!

When someone is in high spirits, inspired and sees opportunities in everything that happens to them this is contagious. When they feel good, more good comes their way. Equally whenever anyone feels like the world is against them then that is all they will see in life.

Even when you are mindful of the thoughts of others, your own thoughts and actions can be influenced by those you surround yourself with. It is your choice whether you surround yourself and be inspired by the success of other business owners. If you choose this you will be encouraged by them and you will then attract success into your life. Alternatively, if you surround yourself with doom and gloom, you may attract this into your life too.

As mentioned in chapter 'Opportunity or Obstacle?' a daily gratitude meditation can be very useful when things happen that we are not happy about. By thanking what has happened, you look at it with a different perspective. Your acceptance of what is going on, allows you to investigate further into why this particular thing could be happening to you.

Accepting an experience allows you to let go of judgement and brings in compassion. This then leads the way to understanding your own thoughts and behaviours.

If you feel like the world is against you then you will always blame someone else for what's happening to you. This doesn't mean that you're responsible for everything that's going wrong in your life. Although, if you are personally involved in all situations then it's time to ask *in what way could you be attributing to this*? How are you responding to it? It is important to bring in compassion here though. It is not about blame or fault finding towards you or anyone else. It is about asking what could be changed.

Remember, you cannot change anyone else. You can only change yourself and that starts with your thoughts, feelings and behaviours. Things will happen in your life that you have no control over, but how you respond to it is your choice. You can choose to see your experiences as frustrating and/or upsetting. Or you can choose to view your experiences as something to learn from and/or as a catalyst for change. Life happens around you, and will keep going long after you are gone. However, your life, and your business, is unique to you and what you do with that is your choice.

Now for some science

What you focus on is what you attract into your life. The good stuff and the bad stuff. This does not mean that what happens to you is what you have asked for but if you think bad stuff will happen to you, then it will. We attract a lot of it through our behaviour and posture.

David Hamilton, author and scientist, spoke at an event of a psychological study where bullies were asked which person they would pick on; a big burly guy or an old woman? Most of them choose the big guy over the slim elderly woman. The reason when asked was because they could tell that the guy was hunched over and looking unsure of himself whereas the woman was upright and appeared to be confident and self-assured.

Science fascinates me because it takes a theory and attempts to prove it, yet it reminds me that everyone has a different perspective.

For example, in the quantum physics world there is a difference of opinion amongst the physicists due to the weirdness of their field and many scientists differ on their belief of what is happening. There have been various attempts by each to explain their rationale behind their belief, even explaining how ridiculous the other belief is, but there is no absolute explanation that everyone agrees on. The point is everyone takes their opinion of what is going on and makes it fit into a perfect explanation. They make their reality fit their beliefs.

If you believe something in your life then this will influence your behaviour, actions and the decisions you make. In science it is called *experimental bias*. This is when a researcher has the potential to influence the results of his/her experiment. This could be either through his/her own behaviour, their choice of words or just simple making the results fit. As a trained hypnotherapist I have also seen how the power of suggestion can influence people. This is why the police, and any good therapist or coach use what is termed *clean language* when asking questions.

In childhood, your brain is a like a sponge and it stays a sponge throughout adulthood but it's more susceptible to other people's opinions and beliefs when younger. Just a simple remark 'Ach he's getting too big for his boots!' can affect how you view someone who is successful for example.

What does 'Ach he's getting too big for his boots!' actually mean?!

I have asked a few people this question, as phrases like this (that are passed down from generation to generation) fascinate me. Most answers are somewhere along the lines of *'that they are thinking something unreasonable, or something impossible and need taken down a peg or too'*. In other words, they should listen to what others are saying or believe instead.

However, the way I see it, is that when someone excels at something it shows something is possible, even if it is just a thought at this stage. I believe it says to everyone else 'Come on, you can do, think or feel this too!'! If you listen to the opinions of others you may not excel, particularly if everyone says it cannot be done!

For example, it was thought to be impossible that a mile could be run in under four minutes. Everyone tried it and failed. Then Roger Bannister came along and broke the record in May 1954, and within six weeks someone else had beaten his record! Yet for nine years everyone thought that the best record was the best that could be done; under four minutes was thought to be impossible!

Top takeaway from this chapter:

Be mindful of how your thoughts and language influence your behaviour and of others in your environment. Listen carefully to those you surround yourself with, and what you read, and question whether you agree or disagree.

INFLUENCING OTHERS

My previous role as a management accountant allowed me to see how organisations can and often will report on results in such a way where it will influence the reader. I am not referring to those who deliberately change the results here, but just by wording something in a certain way, it will encourage the reader to believe or act in a predictable way. The media also do this very well and adverts are very good at this!

Around the 1920's, the marketing world changed dramatically and has remained the same way since. Adverts used to quite factual; i.e. what the product did and/or why it was needed. Sometimes it was just simply a picture of the product and nothing more. Circa 1920, the adverts changed to focus on the worries of the buyers. This was because it was believed (and still thought to be the case) that people are driven by either love, fear or anger, and this encouraged people to buy the product more. Therefore the advert would focus in on how their product would make the buyer more attractive, fitter or happier.

What is the reason I am telling you this?

We are all being influenced every day by others who want us to buy something or believe the same beliefs as them. None of this is ever being done in a manipulative way though. Well, maybe there is a small handful out there but really it is just because we are not being mindful of our actions and thinking for ourselves.

I encourage you to be more mindful of the adverts and conscious of what others say to you, including me! Ask yourself if you really do believe this and what proof do you have that tells you so. More importantly, what outcomes in your business tell you it is true, or not true?

I love psychology because I am fascinated by the behaviour that we adopt when going about our daily lives. I like to think I am very mindful of what I am doing, thinking and feeling. However, every so often I read the results of a psychological study and am surprised at an insight it brings to me. More often than not it gives me clarity into why I do certain things. It can encourage me to change what I'm doing and thinking, but other times it just gives me more of an understanding into what I am doing.

Do your own research

"Don't believe in anything simply because you have heard it. Don't believe in anything simply because it is spoken and rumoured by many. Don't believe in anything simply because it is found written in your religious books. Don't believe in anything merely on the authority of your teachers and elders. Don't believe in traditions because they have been handed down for many generations. But after observation and analysis, when you find that anything agrees with reason and is conducive to the good and benefit of one and all, then accept it and live up to it."

Hindu Prince Gautama Siddharta

Do your own research and experiments. Whenever you feel deflated, sit for a moment or go for a walk and enquire into your thoughts. Ask yourself what are you thinking and then ask where that thought came from. Did it come from an experience or did someone tell you that?

If it was an experience, then what else was going on at the time. What were your thoughts and what was going in your life? If someone told you then consider why they believed that. Who told them, or what experience did they have to make them believe that?

Question the theories that you strongly believe and apply a little science to them. Be curious, shine a light on those beliefs and then do some experiments. It was once thought that the brain was moulded when we were young and then set in stone as we moved into adulthood. However, it has come to light that this was wrong. It has now been proven that the brain is continually shaping itself even after it is fully developed and can even repair itself after damage or use a part of itself that it has never used before. This is called *brain plasticity*.

This also means you can change your behaviours and what you think at any time. I reckon the phrase *'you can't teach an old dog new tricks'* was based on the belief that the brain was set solid once it was developed. This is not true, so what else is false?

This does not mean that it is not challenging to change. It can be difficult to change if we have believed or done something for a long time. It takes conscious effort which is why being mindful of your behaviour and thoughts can help you navigate your way towards your success.

For example, think of yourself walking through the forest following someone who tells you this is the best way to go. The path is clear as this person has walked this way many times. Then one day the person who first introduced you to the forest is not with you and you see a different way and decide to explore it. You make your way through the overgrown part of the forest, and it is tough. You are fighting back the weeds and you keep thinking maybe the other way is shorter or better after all. Maybe that person was right. The new way is really challenging but it is just because you have not carved out the way yet.

Your brain works in exactly the same way (well it's a little more complicated than a forest path but it is a great metaphor!). Your brain creates neuropathways and the more you use them, the more fixed they become. Remember I told you in the introduction the brain likes to use shortcuts and routines to conserve energy, this is how. If you choose another path, your brain forms new neuropathways and over time these get stronger, and the old neuropathways a little weaker, the old forest path becomes overgrown. It is not clear whether the old neuropathway disappears completely in time or not but it does get weaker. It likely depends on the strength of that connection. One day something may cause your brain to follow the old route, we call it an associated trigger in psychology, if you are not mindful of where you are going. Yet over time the new path does becomes your default. It's usually in times of stress or emotional upset that we fall back on our old neuropathways.

For example, a client I had been coaching, picked up her mobile phone that was ringing when she was in the middle of cooking dinner and the kids were running around the house screaming with excitement (as kids do). It turned out to be a new customer and when

Sally was asked her price she defaulted to her old price, the one that was giving her a loss. After Sally had made dinner, eaten and was relaxing in the evening she remembered the price she quoted and got annoyed with herself for not quoting her new price. Yet I reminded Sally of her old path and how we default to these when stressed and asked her to look for the learning in the experience.

After a little soul searching she realised she did learn something valuable in that moment. Never answer the phone when not in a good mental state to conduct business! She also learned that she was too eager to pick up the phone as she wanted to help others yet by being overly keen she had ended up doing this at the expense of her business.

Top takeaway from this chapter:

Experiment with your beliefs. Change them and
notice what changes happen in your business.
Be adventurous but be mindful.

PART 2

What does success really mean for you?

WHAT DO YOU REALLY WANT?

In part one I explained that your beliefs around money come from previous experiences and I encouraged you to ensure that these are positive and will serve your business well. In part two we will explore what beliefs you have about success, and what success actually means for you!

You are energetically drawn in the direction you focus. For example, if you ride a motorbike, you will know that you and your bike will move in the direction you look. For anyone who does not ride a bike, try walking in a straight line with your eyes looking over your left shoulder for one minute. Go on, try it.

If you want to head somewhere you need to be focussed on it.

You must be clear on what you want and avoid thinking too much on what you don't want. Unfortunately, many people will unconsciously set goals on what they wish to avoid in their business eg long hours and a lack of money. If you do this, then that is what you will end up doing. Knowing what you don't want is effective in helping you determine what you DO want (it will usually be the opposite!) although it is only useful during the planning stage. Once you have decided on what you DO want, give that your full attention.

I truly encourage you to tune into your passions and believe that you can create a business out of them. It might get scary but what do you really want? If you really want this, then you have a choice to either go for it 100% or make the odd feeble attempts to achieve it. If you do the latter, you only have yourself to apologise to when you are at the end of your life and you have a list full of regrets.

Do you know what you want?

- Is it financial freedom?
- Is it freedom to do what you want?
- Is it to travel the world?
- Is it flexible hours?
- Is it to spend time with your kids, grandchildren, or elderly parents?
- Or is there something that you have always wanted to do?

I want you to stop for a moment and tune into what you really want out of life. I want you to forget about your business for a moment, and tell me what YOU want. Stop and answer this question before moving on.

Have you done that yet? I'm serious, do it now.

What's your answer?

Still not done, it? Why? What are you afraid to ask for? You might find section three useful, it explores how much you feel worthy of success ie do you feel worthy of asking for what you really want. Let's pretend for now that you do. Go on. Dream you biggest dream. Allow yourself to play this pretend game.

What do YOU really want?

...

Excellent.

Only once you know what you want, can you then answer the following question:

How will your business give you that?

For example, if you want to travel the world, how will your business contribute to this goal? Will it merely provide the money to pay for your holidays or could you bring travel to your business plans?

This is actually a goal one of my clients has and she is working on a business model that facilitates this. Another of my clients determines her business success on being able to spend time with her family, whilst she is able to also provide for them and pay for a degree she never got. Both my book mentor and editor love books and after writing a few themselves they now have a business helping others to write and publish books.

All of them have identified what is important to them; what they truly want (for now at least). Then once they identified that, they opened up their mind to all opportunities that will allow them to have a business than fulfils this desire.

Putting yourself first is not being selfish to your customers. It is the opposite. We'll cover this more in part three but know that when you address your needs before anyone else you interact with the world from a much happier place. You will look for ways to help your customers but within the boundaries of your happiness. If you have ever tried to help someone do something that you really hate, you will know exactly what I mean by this.

If you are not sure how your business could help you with your dream, I want you to list your passions. List everything you enjoy doing. For example, the business owner who wants to spend time with their family looks at their interests. They could get a job in the local supermarket which gives them money to fund their dream (maybe!), but it does not pay for their degree. So they choose to do something that their degree will be on. Something that they are interested in and know a little about, and they will learn even more as they go. It's a win, win situation!

I therefore encourage you now to tune into your passions and believe that you can create a business out of them. If you believe that you cannot, then you will not. Your reality is a mirror of what you believe right now. It might seem scary, I understand that. Perhaps what you are doing just now is safer, but running a business is never a safe bet. Nothing is. Life will continually challenge you.

In my experience, you're better off being challenged when you are having fun and doing something you want to do than when you are just running a business half-heartedly. Trust me I have tried both and so have many of my clients.

What would make your business successful?

Once you have tuned into your passion, you can then align this with your cognitive mind to explore how it will work. If you think about running a business from your logical money mind first, it will not be as successful as it could be until you first bring in your passion.

I listened to my money mind from the age of ten until the moment I launched my business full time. I realised I was not happy doing what I was doing so I quit my job. I made a big mistake though. I ignored my money mind completely and listened to my heart instead. I felt because I had ignored my heart for so long I needed to make up for lost time. This was also quite ironic for an accountant as I was telling others to pay attention to their money but I was ignoring mine!

It was not until my blissful state started to crumble that I panicked and turned down the volume of my heart again, and turned up the volume of my cognitive mind. My business survived but it led me to an unhappy place yet again. It was another eighteen months before I finally understood that I had to listen to them all! I wrote this book, so you don't make the same mistakes I made, and the same as many of the clients who come to me asking for help with their finances do too.

You must engage your money and heart mind together. You need to get them on intimate terms. They need to know what the best way forward for you is, together.

So do you know what would make your business successful, whilst at the same time doing something that you want? Think of your passion, and the things you like to see happen, or maybe it is something that gets you passionately angry and you wish someone could change it? You could be that person!

If you are not sure what you really want, I know some great coaches that can help you gain some clarity. I have listed them in the further resources section. Although you are likely to already have a good idea. The reason you are not allowing yourself to dream it, is because you are coming at it from the cognitive mind first. You need to hold a meeting of the minds and tell the logical part of you to be quiet for a moment and allow your heart and soul to speak. You may find part three helpful in helping you to address this question too.

Believe that you can make it work until your cognitive mind helps you to find the solutions that allow you to do so.

Align the heart and the money mind

Once you have reconnected with your passion, you need to ensure that you are committed to it. If you really want to do this, then do it. It will be tough; you will have the occasionally 'off' day, but let that serve you as a reminder that you are not aligning your head, heart, body and soul. It happens. This is why I talk about setting an intention every day in *12 Steps to Improve Your Cashflow* (and I give you some great tips and share some great resources in part five of this book). You also must be taking care of yourself too, and taking action, but we'll talk about that in parts three and four.

When things show signs of 'going wrong' or something does not feel as blissful as it could be, it is likely because you are either putting something off that appears difficult or there is something that you are thinking or ignoring. I believe running a business is one of the best personal development courses you can do! When something is not going right in your business it is an indication that something is misaligned. You must have your head, heart, body, and soul in harmony before taking action.

I will talk more about looking after your body and taking action later but the head and the heart are the most commonly misalignment. You need to look at your mindset and beliefs, not just with money in general but what you think about money when it comes to listening to your heart.

- What are you thinking?
- What are you imagining?
- What do you really believe?

I coach people on this sort of stuff all the time yet I occasionally find my thinking is out of alignment. I'm only human after all and so are you. If this happens it is important to be compassionate. Remember from part one that your beliefs are just things you have absorbed over time. You can usually uncover a misalignment pretty quickly if you are mindful of your feelings. You may find your happiness fade a little, and perhaps even feel a little grumpy. You may be used to associating grumpiness to a lack of sleep, but I would then encourage you to ask why you are not sleeping very well.

I had a really interesting experience with my first book. I had always wanted to write and it was a passion that I was ignoring. In 2015 I finally did something about it. When *12 Steps to Improve Your Cashflow* went live online the feeling was amazing! Yet within a few minutes I started to feel quite tense and nervous. I went for a walk because I had been working on the final edits for several days and I thought it was just my body crying out for fresh air and exercise. However, soon into my walk I was feeling worse. I then asked myself the questions above and my answers were quite interesting! I'll spare you the details but let's just say that they were not very positive!

There are rare times when a belief escapes me and I just get grumpier. I can occasionally feel overwhelmed and start to believe everything is quite hopeless. This is where my coaches and mentors have been helpful in highlighting what is going on for me. There are times when simply a conversation with a friend or my partner will help too. I encourage you to get a coach and/or meet with a good friend regularly, or take up meditation, or journaling, or all four! Whenever I am getting grumpy about something I stop and take notice. I listen to my thoughts, usually by writing them down and then I start asking myself the kind of questions I would ask a client. Here is a sample:

- What are you thinking?
- Is it a kind thought about you or others? (if you are feeling grumpy, I will take a guess and say you'll answer 'No!' here)
- What does thinking like that give you?
- What does thinking like that not give you?
- What feeling would you like to have instead?
- What thought would give you that feeling?
- What one small thing could you do that would take you closer to that feeling?

Be curious about the answer. You are the only person who can make change happen for yourself.

Top takeaway from this chapter:

Do you believe you can turn your passion into a
business? Do you believe your business can give you
the life you have always dreamed of?
Believe that it is possible.
If you think it is impossible then that is likely why the
cognitive mind will give you multiple reasons
why it is not possible.

Only by believing it is possible will your logical money
mind then be given the signal to start looking for
ways to make money out of it.

WHAT IS YOUR PASSION?

A driver of any vehicle must assess the road in front of him/her and look for any obstacles. They must be focussed, alert and in control. They must take care of their vehicle in order for it to make the journey. If a warning display comes up, then the driver must find a safe place to stop and check the message. Finally, if the driver is on a long journey, they must stop to look at the map or Sat Nav and check their progress to see if they are still heading in the right direction of his/her chosen destination.

As a business owner, you need to keep your eyes open and assess the road in front of you. You must be alert and in control. You must take care of your body for it to last the journey and you must constantly check in with where you want to go.

Most business owners get lost because their belief system starts telling them what to do, or what not to do. This is when it is essential to start listening to your thoughts. You need to make friends with your mind for your business to be successful. This is why I would recommend a meeting of the minds anytime you are feeling a little down and need to make a decision.

Your unconsciousness has absorbed the beliefs of everyone around you, plus a few of your own when you have had a bad day. There are some good ones in there too though, or you would not have had the courage and motivation to start a business in the first place. However, if you allow your unconsciousness to run your business, then you are not in control.

I had one client who told me that she was losing interest in her passion because she was having to do it for money. This told me two things. The most obvious thing was a fear of not having enough money lurking in Tracy's belief system (which is very common with most business owners!). The second was that Tracy was no longer doing what fulfilled her, for the fun of it. This is also very common! She was not engaging her money mind with her heart. Once she did, she felt far better about her business but she was still not taking action. She was afraid. I discuss fear in part four but she was not aligning her heart and cognitive money mind to keep it on course to where she wanted to go.

Aligning your heart with your money mind

Believe that you can make your passion a business and then ask your money mind 'How?'.

Very often we look around us to see what others are doing when it comes to running a business that fits in with a better quality of life, or more time with the family. We brainstorm ways to run a business by listening to our head first, our heart second.

I'm asking you to turn this upside down and consider what you want first. Then brainstorm lots of ways HOW to do.

How can I make this work financially?

Be patient with the answer. It might be the first thing that comes to you, or it might take a few days. It may only come to you step by step. You'll know when it feels right. I cannot give you the magic formula for that, as we are all different, but trust me you will know. Don't ask anyone else at this stage. Not just yet. They will only talk you out of it or tell you what they think. I encourage you to meditate on it first for a few days or weeks, then either just roll it out or then get someone to help you with the finer details of how.

Watch out for guilt

You can either have a business doing something you can do effortlessly yet your heart is really elsewhere, or you can have a business doing something you love doing and it is still effortless! I encourage you to believe you are deserving of a life of fun. Life is not meant to be a struggle. We only think it is when we try to control a misalignment with our minds.

Guilt is a common response when it comes to earning more money than just enough, or having 'too much' fun. I had a client who had overheard her father saying that she and her sister should be ashamed of all the presents they get, when there were so many poor unlucky kids in the neighbourhood. Martina then felt guilty from that moment on anytime anything was going good in her life, particularly financially. It is no surprise that she didn't have very much money to pay her bills each month. She felt guilty if she was even remotely financially comfortable ie able to afford a holiday. The only way she was able to move on was to acknowledge that the guilt she was feeling was her fathers. She was far too young to know any better and it was her father who was the one buying all the presents. She still felt she wanted to help others so we explored how she could do that, as well as keep her own family financially safe.

I reminded her though that most people who are poor (and I was once one of them) don't actually want handouts. Handouts embarrass them. They just want an opportunity to fulfil their potential. We may at times in our life need support but I also believe we can get lazy if others do too much for us. Since meeting my partner, he takes care of my car. I no longer check my water, oil, battery, or even when my MOT is due as he has it all in hand. I used to check my car on a weekly basis before I met him. I have got lazy when it comes to servicing my vehicle because I know he will do it for me. However, we are part of a team now and he leaves all the food shopping to me and is not bothered what I cook for dinner. We have come to rely on each other for something that we did ourselves before we met.

Some things do make sense to rely on others for, especially if someone excels at something better than you. I believe it is about having a balance of being supportive of others but supporting yourself as well. However, I do recommend practicing gratitude for situations like this too.

Top takeaway from this chapter:

Follow your passion, but listen to your money mind too. Believe you are worth it and feel comfortable with your achievements. Do not give into guilt. Turn it into gratitude and motivation to inspire and give opportunities to others.

HOW WILL YOU RECOGNISE SUCCESS?

Hopefully by now you will have an idea what success means to you. This chapter will really help you to get clear on what it looks like. Understand that what you deem to be success will change throughout your life so this exercise is good to do every three to twelve months.

- What does your success look like?
- What does your success feel like?
- What does your success sound like?
- How will you recognise it?

When you set a goal, you are only able to assess how well you have achieved that goal by setting markers to guide you. For example, if you ever had a goal to lose weight you would have had a number of markers. You would have known how well you were doing, either by what the scales told you, how much energy you had, the looseness of how your clothes felt and how quickly you got your breath back after climbing a flight of stairs.

You need to apply this same procedure in your business. Once you have connected in with your passion, your purpose and why you are in business, you need to identify a handful of markers that will let you know how well you are doing in terms of you path to success. These will guide you on a day to day basis.

These will be the signposts that you can assess how your day has been with regards to your purpose and what makes you feel good about yourself and your business.

List at least nine things that you want to achieve in any given day, week or month that link to your passion, your values and your business. They will include financial information such as your sales and profit for the month, but the majority of these will include non-financial information.

Your intentions (financial and non-financial targets) will be linked to what you really want from your life and your business. The reason for doing this is to check in to see if you are fulfilling your purpose every day and feel fulfilled that you have contributed to your success today. This is the essential ingredient to a successful business.

Sales, money in the bank, and profit are all important to your business to ensure its existence in this world, but your business is not just about existing. You could survive on water, a little food and sit doing nothing all day. You would be surviving, and often we find ourselves in this state when we are ill. However, when you feel good, you have the energy to make your mark on the world. That is what you and your business need to do. Leave the world your legacy.

To help you with this exercise, I share mine below. These will give you an indication of what we will cover in the rest of this book and how you too can have a successful business doing what you love and be happy about it! Feel free to borrow them or use them to help you come up with your own.

Helen's Daily Success Intentions
- Have I been authentic, present and trusted in the moment today?
- Have I read, meditated and written today?
- Have I had fun today?
- Have I told someone I care about, that I love them today?
- Have I smiled and said hello to a stranger today?
- Have I shown compassion to myself and to others today?
- Have I shown respect to my finances and my body today?
- Reflection – if no to any of the above, why not and what can I learn from this if anything?

Helen's Weekly Success Intentions
- Have I given myself time to rest in the evenings?
- Have I given my partner my attention this week?
- Have I met up with a family member or a friend this week?
- Have I given 18hrs of my available working time to my clients, 7hrs to business development and 3hrs to admin and finances this week?
- Reflection – if no to any of the above, why not and what can I learn from this if anything?

Helen's Monthly Financial Success Intentions
- Have I made my monthly sales target this month?
- Have I made monthly profit target this month?
- Reflection – if no to any of the above, why not and what can I learn from this if anything?
- What can I invest in next month with my profit that will grow my business and me?

I encourage you to do yours now. Even if you just list three for each and then come back to these as you read through the book.

My Daily Success Intentions are:

- ✓ Have I ....
- ✓ Have I ....
- ✓ Have I ....

Reflection – if no to any of the above, why not and what can I learn from this if anything?

My Weekly Success Intentions are:

- ✓ Have I ....
- ✓ Have I ....
- ✓ Have I ....

Reflection – if no to any of the above, why not and what can I learn from this if anything?

My Monthly Financial Success Intentions are:

- ✓ Have I ....
- ✓ Have I ....
- ✓ Have I ....

Reflection – if no to any of the above, why not and what can I learn from this if anything?

Reflections

You will have noticed that I added in a reflections question in mine and yours. This is because in order for you to achieve success you will have to assess the feedback.

For example, if we think of the person losing weight. They will only know what is working and what is not working by trying different things then assessing their mini targets. This is what we must do in our business too. Focus on your goal yet equally measure the feedback and make tweaks when necessary.

If we fixate on meeting our goals, particularly by a given date, we are inviting stress in. This is why I prefer to call them intentions. One of my mentors taught me a simple yet life changing technique. On days when you are feeling overwhelmed, identify just one thing that you MUST do that day, and acknowledge that everything else can wait. When Avril first suggested it, I thought she was mad! However, after a couple more weeks of mental exhaustion from the stress and the physical exertion of attempting to do it all, I did what she suggested. The feeling that came from doing that single most important thing that mattered to me was empowering. I still had to adopt a few time management techniques which I share in part five but it gave me energy to do so much more.

I still adopt this principle even two years on and it came in particularly useful when writing this book. A second project had started before I was finished writing this book, and my gran, who lived seventy-five miles away, was not well. This was all on top of business as normal. I remembered Avril's wise words and on some days my intention was to just simply be present and trust in the moment.

However, by focusing on just that one thing each day, I found energy on some days to do more than I initially thought I could manage. This was all done without pushing my body to the extreme which was something I joked with my current mentor. After I asked Karen if she had any tips to get more out the day, I realised that I was not taking care of myself. This is something that must always be aligned to your success, but more on that in part three.

The reason why your daily decisions must be aligned to your vision

I read about a study in the book *Coaching with NLP* by Joseph O'Connor and Andrea Lages that was carried out on medium sized companies across Europe, about fifteen years ago. The results showed that 95% of EVERDAY business decisions **disagreed** with business strategy.

This is why it is important that you know what you want to do in your business. It is important to know what it is that you are passionate about because life will throw things at you. You are human which means you have chemicals (some natural, and possible some man-made depending on what you consume) running around your body. You have emotions too and you have an over-active mind. These are all great ingredients for a crap day! For example, I have noticed that alcohol and sugar, affect my mood considerably, and being a woman my hormones go a bit crazy every four weeks!

If you are doing something that you are truly passionate about then this will really help you on these days. However, if you have ever dragged yourself through one of these days to do a job that you didn't care about then you will know exactly what I mean!

Ensure that every day you know your *Why,* what your values are and what drives you forward, then set your intentions on all the choices and decisions you have to make today. This will steer your business in the direction you want to go. If you don't do this, then you could end up somewhere else entirely! Maybe you will be happy about that though - it is always your choice.

I certainly encourage you to be compassionate about the paths you do venture down and maybe there is something to learn. If you feel your soul is pulling you in one direction, don't ignore it, but instead find the courage to believe in it.

Top takeaway from this chapter:

Would you drive a car with your eyes closed? Would you ignore the warning lights from the dashboard? Identify what is important to you and how this could be aligned with your business. What things make you feel good? Identify your passions and set daily, weekly and monthly intentions to help you stay on course.

PART 3

Do you feel worthy of success?

IS IT TRUE THAT WE SHOULD WORK HARD, PLAY LATER?

In part one I asked you to consider being ok with money in your life, yet equally not fearing it. In part two, I asked you what success would look like for you and your business. In part three I am going to ask what you would feel if you achieved that success. Do you deserve a successful business or are you beating yourself up over something that happened years ago? Have you achieved success in the past only to dismiss it saying it was luck or the result of hard work? Do you think you are only worthy of success if you work hard and are exhausted at the end of each day?

You could achieve success by putting a lot of hours in, however that also depends on what success means to you. If success means spending time with your family now, then working long hours will NOT give you that.

It is a common myth that business success will make you spend less time with your kids/ family. This is a belief that is engrained into our subconscious in our society. It is important that you understand that success itself will not make anyone do anything. It is like money. It is about the meaning you give it.

Each of us chooses what we do. We may have an underlying belief that we have to work all hours to be successful, but that too is just a belief. In part two I encouraged you to think about what you want success to look like (ie what do you really want). If you don't want it to be long hours away from your family, then it doesn't have to be that way. Success is whatever you want it to be.

I had a client, who was challenged with this belief after her father spent most of his time away working in his business when she was younger. As a child Gemma rarely saw him. She believed that lots of money and a successful business meant no time with her children. Gemma was not prepared to do this, as her children meant the world to her, and as a result she was struggling financially. After we looked at her father's behaviour and then explored what Gemma believed success to be, we finally got to the bottom of what she wanted and why she was struggling with it.

Gemma wanted to spend time with her kids and have a successful business. Because of her father's actions she had believed money meant no time with her kids but that had been her father's choice. Admittedly it was not pleasant to acknowledge that her father had chosen to spend time working, away from her and her brothers and sisters. However, once she accepted this Gemma was able to change her belief about what success meant and then started asking how she can achieve a successful business in addition to a successful life (ie time with her family).

Another difference I have observed between a successful businesses and unsuccessful one is the successful businesses and its owner(s) know how to have fun. Successful business owners ensure every day has some fun it. That is why you see the top CEO's on the golf course, having a long lunch with their friends, or flying their private jets.

A successful entrepreneur I observed a few years ago started their day early with the gym, then breakfast with his young family. He then went into the office and dealt with a few phone messages and emails, followed by a couple of meetings before chilling with his family when they got back from school. He fitted his business around his family and the lifestyle he wanted. I have seen this so many other times before from other successful business owners. They invest in themselves and the lifestyle they want. They work around their life. Work does not insist on how often they see their family. They insist on work fitting in with their family and they still make it successful.

The mistake unsuccessful business owners make is putting off their own personal success to make room for their business success. They delay having fun until holidays or special occasions. They work twelve or more hours a day, exhaust themselves, have a holiday to recharge their batteries, yet never fully switch off as they are still checking their emails and phone messages daily, then come back feeling a little refreshed but still exhausted.

I was once like that and I am sure you will resonate with it too.

I worked non-stop building my business at the beginning mainly because I believed that I had to work hard to get what I wanted, primarily because it was what worked in the past to get results. What I ignored was it also brought me less time with my friends and family, less time reading and writing and it also brought me ill-health. Time with my friends, family, reading, writing and good health were all things that made my personal life successful.

Through working fourteen hours a day, my business was successful in that I had plenty of clients to keep me busy, in fact I was at the point when I was turning clients away. I was bringing in a decent profit but I didn't feel successful. I felt exhausted. I had not seen my friends in months and dinners were rushed with my partner.

After a very stressful month, I decided things had to change. I thankfully had the sense to look for an employee. I had to put my own life and wellbeing first.

I still believed that success was in a direct correlation to profits, even more now I had the additional costs of salary and rental of an office. After a couple of conversations with some friends I realised I didn't have much fun in my life (which was something else I associate with success). That was when I looked back at the lives of successful business owners, gained hope, experimented and this book was born.

I asked myself what success would look like, just like I asked you in part two. I was shocked to uncover that success was in within my reach but I had chosen to block it due to the myth of having to work long hours and reap the rewards later. I had worked seven days a week since I was ten years old. I was knackered. I truly didn't know if I had the energy to last another five years when I will have paid off the mortgage.

I reconnected to my soul and instead of just making time for reading, writing, and connecting with my partner a couple of times a week I made a conscious effort to do these things daily. My day now has more fun in it, hence why I have these as daily intentions that you read in part two. My health has significantly improved too! These help remind me how I recognise success. I know I can't spend money until I have it and the same applies to my energy levels. I can't do anything for anyone else until I have nourished my soul (ie charged my batteries). The more nourished I feel, the more energy I have and the more fun I have in my life and business.

You too need to invest in your health and your soul before you can give to others. If you are not aligned, then it is likely life will be more challenging than it needs to be. When your mind, heart, body and soul are in harmony you will find that life works with you and is no longer against you. Everything seems to work out better and more smoothly. There will still be a few hiccups that you have no control over but you will respond differently.

From a money perspective, you take better control of your finances and you realise you no longer need something you thought you could not live without. Additionally, sales come to you more effortlessly as well. If you are happy and successful, you attract more customers. If you are exhausted not many people will want to work with you. If you are energetic, everyone wants to work with you!

Additionally, when your head, heart, body and soul are aligned you will find support and trust is more evident. The things you do are more natural and seem to contribute to the bigger picture of your business with ease. That is why the deals get made on the golf course or at social gatherings. Businesses are having fun because they are aligned. They are getting sales too because their head, heart, body and soul are aligned.

My clients often come to me because they feel they need to change, yet they fear not having enough money to pay the bills. They want to know how they can do this and have enough money. I get them to see their money differently, as I explained in part one. We identify what success would look like to them, as I explained in part two, and how they could add more fun into their lives. We then get to work on identifying what beliefs are preventing their success.

We do this through a number of techniques but primarily we look at the feedback their business is giving them. Your business will always mirror something to you that is not aligned. If you are not getting sales or you are struggling financially then your business is asking you to realign. I believe you are ignoring something in your life, something that one or more of your minds is trying to tell you.

If you are currently challenged right now, I encourage you to answer the following:

- What are you ignoring in your life that keeps calling to you?
- What could you do that could help your business but you are not doing?
- What could you do that could help your health but you are not doing?
- What are you thinking or feeling that is not helping your mood?
- What could you do that would make you happy but you are not doing?
- Is there something in your personal life that you are ignoring?
- What is it that you are doing that you would have to give up if you aligned your head, heart, body and soul?

Every client has a different set of beliefs and frustrations. Some overlap such as the associations of money and success, but generally speaking everyone has their own unique view of the world. However, mostly every client always comes back to same core belief: how much they believe they are worthy of the success they truly desire. This is further broken down to how much they love and value themselves.

You may not see the signs so prominently in your personal life but you will listen when the sales are not coming in or you have no money in your bank account!

Do you love yourself, or do you put your family, friends and business before your own happiness? What one small step could you take that would say 'I love me!'? If that is too far a step, as it was for one of my clients, how about asking "What would you do if you loved yourself?" Be curious as to what pops into your thoughts.

Top takeaway from this chapter:

Do you believe that you have to earn success by putting yourself through some sort of pain, usually working long hours away from those you love? Could you consider there being another way. Align your idea of success with your money mind and believe it is possible to have fun doing so.

DO YOU VALUE YOURSELF?

If you sacrifice time with your family/friends or work late into the night, only to rise earlier the next day then you may feel you have earned success. What if you were to just wake up and be successful, without any conscious effort at all?

I have had clients recover from severe illnesses beat themselves up that they are unable to get up very early in the morning and need to take a wee nap in the day. Why were they unable to acknowledge that waking up every day and going to work is a success? Why were they unable to work only a few hours a day and be happy about that? It was because they felt, like mostly everyone else, that they have to work morning, noon and night.

Most business owner, when asked how many hours they work, reply circa twelve hours a day, seven days a week, (by the time you include emails and admin). What amazes me is that anyone who works four days a week always says they work part-time!

I believe our success is about the quality of the time we put in. Not quantity, but quality. Four or six hours a day of feeling good and refreshed are far more productive than twelve hours rushed and frazzled. Alternatively working twelve hours for three or four days and then taking the rest of the week off might also work for you. If you have a consultancy or coaching business, income is very dependent on your time, which is why the right price is essential and passive income is also advised. (NB: Passive income is when a product/service can be sold over and over again with very little effort. Examples include online courses, books, affiliate income.)

If you allow yourself to have time out to relax, exercise and spend time with your family or friends, then you will work far better than if you just dragged yourself through the day. The secret is to allow yourself to have that time out. That means you have to give yourself a bit of love. No-one is making you work all these hours. If you are not making a profit, then you really must look at your prices. However, you will feel uncomfortable putting your prices up if you don't value yourself.

How much are you worth?

In the finance world, a person's net worth is valued based on their business net worth (ie assets and cash, less debts). However, this is only a measure for financial success, not true success. This can be seen when people achieve financial success yet don't feel successful. At least thirty-two million people in the UK buy a lottery ticket on average three times a week. Some of these people become millionaires, yet some of the winners lose all their money between one and two years. This is because of two reasons. Primarily, due to the fact that they don't know what to do with their millions other than spend it. Secondly, it is because they thought that money was what they wanted but really it was something much more.

In part two I asked you to really consider what you want. I don't know how you got on but some of my clients struggle with this question. To answer what they really want meant putting themselves first. This meant loving themselves.

Do you serve others in the day before taking care of your own needs?

Do you fix everyone's breakfast before sitting down to have your own? Do you focus on getting all you work done in a day before putting your feet up and relaxing? If you have children, you likely see to them before you fix your own dinner or do everything for them before relaxing. However, like one of my clients, I advise you to wake up a little early and give yourself some 'me time' first. I do this and I don't have kids! The cat gets fed whilst my coffee is brewing then I sit and meditate or read for at least thirty minutes before my partner wakes up.

Are you flexible with your customers on when they come to see you or are you strict about your appointment times? It is good to have a little flexibility for your customers but only if it suits you and your life. If you only get to spend time with your kids or friends in the evenings and weekends, then you have the choice of not working those times. This means loving yourself before your customers.

If all this stuff scares you, how about you consider just putting yourself first one day a week, or doing something you enjoy first thing. I had a client who loved playing computer games. Jane really craved this first thing in the morning but fought the urge to do it. She would often find herself pushing through her day. I did this too before I started to read in the morning.

I encouraged her to allow herself to play the games for two mornings a week, then resist the urge the other two mornings in the week. On the fifth morning I asked her to assess her productivity on the days she played the games against her productivity on the days she didn't play the games. She was then to choose the most productive start to the day for the fifth day.

What do you think was the most productive start for her? The day she played the computer games for thirty minutes in the morning or the days she did not. It turned out she was far more productive when she gave herself a little of what she craved and played the computer games.

Top takeaway from this chapter:

Do you put yourself first?
Consider starting your day with something you
enjoy doing first thing in the morning?

WHY DO YOU TREAT YOURSELF?

When we lack self-love we often try to make up for it by giving ourselves 'treats'. We think we are loving ourselves by giving ourselves the treats but in reality we are just masking the truth. This can also have a negative impact on our health and finances.

Some people spend excessively and buy things to make them feel better; cakes, sweeties, alcohol, clothes, gadgets, holidays. These things are all nice to have in moderation but those who spend excessively and have a 'self-love deficit' will buy them frequently.

A coffee and a cake is a lovely treat once every couple of weeks but when does it become too often? When does it become a substitute for self-love? When do the clothes purchased and frequent new cars become more than just a necessity? Once you come from a place of self-love you can still enjoy these things but you will save lots of money if you love yourself and put yourself first.

Too much is a lack of self-love but so is none at all

It is traditional to think that if you need to save money you must cut back on all expenditure. However, if you cut back on the treats, ie on the things that make you feel better, then you are in for a rough ride. Either that or you will give up pretty quickly!

It is like dieting. Any good weight loss coach will advise you to eat a little of what you like because that is the only way the diet will be successful. If you make attempts at saving money before you feel even the tiniest bit of self-love, then you will just feel even worse! You can save money and still buy these things, just less frequently.

The real reason you buy stuff

I explained earlier in part one how adverts can influence what you buy and why you buy it. The marketing guys know you want to feel better about your life or that you want to feel more attractive if you are looking for a relationship. They do this to encourage you to buy their products. They are giving you something you are asking for.

You can feel better about yourself without buying clothes, gadgets or food. When you love yourself, you will still buy these, just less often, and when you do you will value them more.

What has this to do with business success?

How you feel about money and how you feel about yourself, will determine how you interact with your customers. You may think that by hiding behind emails and a website you would not have to worry about that but be assured that the message in spilling out somehow!

I always encourage my clients to tune into what they are thinking, feeling and/or imagining when they buy something or when they are discussing their prices. This tells them how they are really feeling in the moment. It's a bit like a mindfulness practice but in relation to your money and business growth. If you do this, you will start to understand the reason why you buy and whether you are just doing it to feel better or look good in front of people.

Additionally, if you feel uncomfortable talking about your prices it means that you don't value what you have to give your customers. If you don't value it, then neither will they.

What could you have done instead?

When you choose to buy something, it means you are unable to use that money to buy something else. For example, for every unnecessary treat you buy now, you move further away from your financial freedom goal. Every time you choose to work late, you move further away from your 'I want to see my family/friends more' goal. Every time you do something you don't want to do, you are moving further away from what you really want.

This is why it is crucial that you identify what you really want, which is what I discussed in part two. Once you establish what you really want, you are more focussed on achieving that and you do not spend your time or money on something that does not give you that.

I would be interested to know what intentions you came up with part two. I shared my own to give you an indication that I believe true success is about nourishing our soul, loving ourselves and being a better person to those around us. To run a business, it needs sales. To grow a business, it needs profits. To grow your business naturally and with ease, it needs your self-love.

This is why, when I coach my clients to improve their relationship with money, we also work on the relationship they have with themselves and others. Money is a form of love. By not looking after your money you are not looking after yourself.

If I have not looked at my bank account or recorded my expenses within a week I start to feel agitated and unbalanced, just as I would if I was not looking after myself by having a good night's sleep, meditated, read or wrote daily.

If you love yourself then you are always looking after yourself, mentally, physically, emotionally and spiritually. If you are going through a tough time emotionally or physically then you do need to go that extra mile. If you are feeling ill, you will likely consider a day off, or a morning at least, treating yourself to a day on the sofa reading a book or watching a film to recharge your energy. If you apply the same strategy to money when you are feeling low about money (ie not having enough) then the last thing you should be doing is ignoring it or believing that things will get better through chance.

Have you ever felt a cold coming on, ignored it and just kept going? Then, before long you collapsed in a heap when you ran out of energy? If you ignore your finances for long enough, you will also collapse in a heap when you run out of money.

Top takeaway from this chapter:

Do you love yourself enough to look after you finances? Are your financial decisions aligned with your good intentions only to fall flat on bad day when you need a pick-me-up?

WHAT CAN THE VALUE WE HAVE OF OURSLEVES TELL US ABOUT PRICING?

When you love yourself, you value yourself more. When you value yourself more, you know what you are worth. When you know your worth, you know what to charge and feel comfortable doing so.

Your price says a lot about what you think you are worth to others. I am talking about your true *worth*, not just what you have in the bank or in assets. However, interestingly, there is often a correlation as to how much someone loves themselves and how much money they have, or assets they have. I have overheard many people comment that a certain businessman or actress loves themselves. They say it in jest but I believe that it is true. They are doing what they love and they are charging a price that reflects their own self-worth. Sadly, though, a lot of people associate self-love with being selfish. This is another myth!

Self-love is about respecting yourself. It is about looking after yourself before you look after others. A battery is unable to charge anything if its energy is depleted. You are no different. As I mentioned earlier, when you fly anywhere the air host(ess) reminds you that if anything happens in the plane, you must put on your oxygen mask before helping others. Is this being selfish? No because you can only save people when you are alive and healthy!

Increasing your self-love increases your success and personal worth.

How much is your happiness worth to you and to your family? Do you remember the accountant I mentioned in part one who paid £7,000 for a coach to help him improve his health? He improved his health and his outlook in life as well as finding a beautiful wife and having two adorable children. That was an act of self-love that led to a successful family life and a successful business.

When I see people undercharging, I find there is often a link between what they are charging and how unhappy they are with their life/business. In the past, during pricing conversation with my clients they often ended the conversation saying *'OK, I will tell my customers, my accountant has told me to increase my prices'*. I used to laugh at this and say *'If that helps!'* but now I challenge them on this. It intrigues me that some business owners don't feel confident about putting their prices up and therefore have to 'hide' behind their accountant in order to feel good about the increased price. I am pretty sure that is why most accountants get a raw deal!

Remember that it is always your choice whether your charge the recommended price that your accountant or finance coach suggests. Although bear in mind there is unlikely to be much of a business remaining if you continue to run at a loss, which is what is really being highlighted.

The main priority of all accountants is to look after your business and ensure that it fulfils its purpose. Your accountant is on your side and wants to help but you do have to start valuing yourself and thinking with the head, heart, body and soul minds aligned. Connect with your purpose to remind yourself why you are in business every day and ensure you have the resources to reach all your ideal customers. Put yourself first and love yourself.

Do you think you're not good enough?

David Hamilton's latest book *I Heart Me* tells the reader that he felt he was not good enough and only through loving himself more was he able to believe that he was good enough. This was a subject that resonated with me due to my own experiences and I recognise it in so many of my clients.

"We put others' success down to money or position ... But great things are often achieved by people who started with nothing – and holding back is almost always down to a feeling of NOT enough. (p202).

Loving ourselves is NOT being selfish. Only by loving and valuing ourselves can we give the world our best.

If you don't value yourself then it's likely you will not value other people either. If you don't value yourself, you will undercharge and underestimate your skills, and you will expect others to undercharge too, as well as undervalue their skills. When you're doing this, you are de-valuing your gift to the world and you are de-valuing the gifts others have brought to this world. This is why clients who are undercharging attract customers who don't value themselves either.

When a client told me that she didn't believe she could make a profit, I asked her why. Suzy responded by saying it was because she didn't think anyone would pay the new price we had calculated together. After I asked a few more questions we discovered it was because she didn't think she was good enough. After a couple of sessions, where we explored how she could love herself more, Suzy soon felt more confident to increase her price. The most amazing part is that Suzy's new customers didn't question her price and this really surprised her. I explained that this was because they could see the true value that Suzy was giving them now that she was coming from a place of self-love herself.

Let go of the need to please everyone. Say *'No'* once in a while.

I don't believe I was alone when my biggest weakness was saying 'Yes' to everyone. I learnt that your business, and you, will suffer if you are not honest about what you can and cannot do. My life and my business improved after I began nourishing my soul and saying 'No'.

When I said 'Yes' to everything that was offered to me, I didn't think about (a) when I could fit it in, nor (b) if I wanted to do it. To be fair not many jobs came my way that I disliked, but there were certainly times I said 'Yes', when I should have said 'No'.

Once when I was exhausted from trying to help so many people, my mentor advised me to say 'No', even if I then changed my mind later on. It was challenging at first as I felt bad about it, however it turned out everyone was happy to wait until I had availability. Those who had urgent requests, either managed ok, or found someone else to help in the short term, but they still wanted to work with me.

What if you know you should say *'No'*, but somehow you still say *'Yes'*?

The reason you may be challenged with the word 'No' is because you have associated it as a negative thing. We all remember as a child having fun, when our teachers and parents would shout *'No, Stop that!'* and being told *'No'* when we wanted something.

Think of what happens when you do this with your own children, your friend's children, or even a pet. Do they accept gracefully and walk away or do they plead, throw a tantrum and/or sulk?

Some people associate the word 'No' with angry or distressed people. This is often why sometimes it can be uncomfortable with saying 'No', for fear that they will be hurting or upsetting the other person. This is highly unlikely, unless they are five years old...

Adults understand that not everything can be done immediately. If it is urgent they may go and find someone who can help them but if they like your service or products, they will come back. Acknowledge that 'No' does not always mean that someone will get upset. If they do, your health is far more important, and I would ask you to consider if you really want them as a customer?

Top takeaway from this chapter:

Do what you can but don't over promise.
Always put yourself first. Value yourself and
your gifts. You are good enough.

BELIEVE IN YOURSELF AND BE YOU!

A few months after I went full-time in my business, the honeymoon period started to wear off and I began doubting what I was doing. For quite some time I'd wanted to give the business my full attention and enjoy my life again. I was having lunch in the garden, wearing my jeans to work, and meeting lots of interesting people. However, after another day of no sales, in addition to the increased frustration at my partner greeting me with *'Did you get any more clients today?'* the cloud descended on me and I considered chucking it all in.

I went so far as applying for a job and going to the interview, but then I realised I wanted to keep running the business. I just had to find the motivation and strength to do so. I remembered the main reason I wanted to start my business was to spend time with friends and family, especially my gran. Additionally, my mum had just had an operation and I was grateful to spend some time helping her - so I struggled on with the business and I got a few more clients but still not enough.

My mum went back to work and I ran out of positive things to discuss with my gran and friends. A cold winter arrived and I got the flu, so I had to rest and stop going to all the networking meetings I'd been attending. I felt better by Christmas and was able to catch up with one of my best friends on Boxing Day. As I was running about her house playing with my godson, I realised I'd not had much fun lately, flu aside. Later over a glass of wine, my friend helped me realise that I was trying to be what I thought was expected of me. I was actively trying be someone I was not.

I was selling myself as a stereotypical accountant but that was most definitely not what I was. As a result, I was tense, and not relaxed with the people at networking events. I was not writing blogs or in my journal and I was not saying anything that was remotely personal on my business social media page. I could've been anyone. I didn't stand out.

As I was switching off the Christmas lights that night I caught a glimpse of a few opened presents under the tree and immediately felt a rush of gratitude towards my partner. He'd bought me a multipack of notebooks and said whilst I was opening them *"I know you like writing and I have not seen you write in a while"*. He'd acknowledged my love of writing yet I had clearly forgotten who I was. The second reminder of the day!

I spent the rest of holidays doing what I love. Writing and learning. I even spent a whole day learning how to calculate some physics equation! Why? Because I enjoyed it and it made me happy. By the 4th January I was feeling like me again and ready for a call that provided me with an opportunity that saved my business.

This is why I believe doing what you love affects your business. I have many more examples from my life, and my clients, but this was the most profound. Perhaps it was luck or maybe it was just a random opportunity, but I know the 'me' before Christmas would have spoken differently on the call, and acted very different in the meeting.

It is important that you are YOU. Alisoun Mackenzie was the first person who encouraged me to be authentic and now a lot of personal development books will tell you the same - yet I didn't realise just how much it mattered until I was not being me. I wanted to wear formal casual wear, but I felt I should still wear a suit jacket when I went to networking events to show I was a professional accountant. I didn't show my weirdness; my love of geeky things because I thought my profession was geeky enough and I wanted people to like me. I didn't express my openness of things such as reiki and spirituality because I felt that would again undermine my qualification. I didn't tell people that I love learning things just for fun because I thought they would not take me seriously.

If you have always been someone else, being yourself may be a challenging path to walk at first. You will have good days and you will off days. Just keep bouncing back. It will soon become the norm. Even now, every so often I trip up. I'm human and psychological experiments have proven that on occasion, people will do or say whatever everyone else is doing or saying.

Being different means you will be noticed. You do have to be comfortable with that. That is almost a book on its own, and in fact there are many books out there to help you with confidence. What you need to know is that it is about trusting who you are and what excites you, and having plenty of practice. A book cannot tell you how to do that, other than some of what I have covered. Another suggestion would be to start by showing strangers in the supermarket or on the street more of the real you, and then bring that into your business if that helps.

Whenever I start doubting this I remind myself to trust my intuition. I surround myself with others who are similar to me; those who believe in doing things differently, even from each other.

Be grateful and do the things you love doing

No matter how small a gift is, cheap, or unpractical it is (like an illness!) be grateful for it. There is a quote that I love that says:

"*When a child gives you a gift, even if it is a rock they just picked up, exude gratitude. It might be the only thing they have to give and they have chosen to give it to you.*" – *Dean Jackson*

I believe your business and life is that child.

Your business might not be exactly the way you want it right now, but it is always giving from a place that it can. If you stand back long enough to appreciate what you've been given, then you'll see something truly wonderful in that gift.

Do the things you love doing because then you shine. You will get a real buzz out of it, you are happier and that improves your mood. You will be better equipped to deal with what life and your business throws at you. That is what successful business owners do. They do the things that excite them.

Sometimes, depending on your experiences in life and even just the lives of those around, you might feel guilty if you are having too much fun. You may have been told life is hard and is to be taken seriously. I disagree. Life is what you make it.

Certainly there will be very challenging times (I've had a few!) and tough choices to make but that doesn't mean you should sit in self-pity. Anyone who has ever had a serious illness, or experienced a family member or friend die, will know just how short our life can be. Sometimes nature will take it away from us, sometimes it can be because we are in the wrong place at the wrong time.

The fact is we are all going to die. If you are lucky it will be when you are nearing hundred years old and you have run out of ideas for having fun. Run your business the way you want it to be run. Do things you love doing. Quirky things that bring a smile to your face or make you chuckle so much that it hurts. If you cannot think of anything, go spend some time with a mischievous elderly person or child. I know a few if you're stuck!

Giving your true self to the world is the greatest gift you can give your customers, your family, your friends and you!

Be honest about who is behind your business

You should be honest about who you are and what you do. Let your customers know who they will be dealing with and what they will get, just like you'd expect your suppliers to be with you.

I understand that some businesses like to appear bigger than one person or a small number of employees, especially if their customer is a large business. However, I encourage you to let your customers know who is really behind the business. Most businesses and people like to know who they are buying from. Social media, newsletters and books can be a great channel for this.

I worked from home initially because it kept my costs down whilst I got my business established, which is something I encourage any start-ups (ie keep costs low). I know others now who work from home to fit in with their childcare. I used to shy away from telling people this though in case it made me sound unprofessional. I soon realised I was not being authentic, I was holding information back because of my own perception of professionalism.

If you pretend you are someone you are not, customers will see right through it, and if they don't straight away then they will be disappointed when they finally do. They will wonder what else you've lied about.

Never shy away from who you are. Use social media to let the world see who and what you are passionate about. Technology is moving so fast that we forget that there are humans behind every business. Let the world see the people behind yours.

It's so easy in today's world to hide behind a computer and almost have your business running on auto pilot. It does allow the owner to have more flexibility over their life but I truly feel that we should be communicating on a personal level more rather than less. Many science experiments have proved that psychical connections are good for our health.

Be Compassionate and Authentic

At the time of writing this book, there is an international drive to encourage women on company boards. I feel this has been slightly taken out of context. Some are looking at it from a gender perspective and claiming its fair on both sexes. I feel it is because it is recognised that women in general have a more compassionate viewpoint on decisions and this is becoming more and more important to the business world.

There are certainly more business magazines and books now than a decade ago, telling you to treat your staff with more respect, be environmentally friendly, and be kind to everyone you interact with. However, how many readers believe them? How many business owners and managers are willing to take that leap of faith? Perhaps more truthfully, how many wish they could be compassionate but are getting hassle from their boss, the board of directors, shareholders or customers?

The truth is you have to take a leap of faith. If you truly are a compassionate being, you will never be happy until you are in your business too. You will find in time, you will be respected, trusted, and encouraged. You will be given far more opportunities than ever before, all for being just you; compassionate and authentic. It will also reduce your stress levels and that in itself will make you a more compassionate person.

Being yourself is the easy bit. The challenge is to be confident enough to be yourself. This will only come when you do it over and over again. There is no magic formula on how to do this. Trust me I have looked! There are some great supportive coaches out there though who will help you.

Top takeaway from this chapter:

Accept the gifts your business and life give you.
Be yourself and shine.
Be compassionate to others.

SCHEDULE TIME IN THE DAY FOR YOUR MOST IMPORTANT CUSTOMER

Most people think their customers are the important ones in their business, and they are very important but YOU are the most important person in your business.

I personally believe that it is vital that you get a good night's sleep, remain calm and balanced and are able to focus on every task. You shouldn't be rushing about stressed, arguing with your partner, juggling three things at the same time then falling into a crumbled heap at bedtime, only to get up four hours later because your mind just will not stop thinking or doubting. Trust me, tried that too!

I have come to realise that if I try and cram too much into my day I don't sleep very well and the next day I can feel the stress building up. However, by giving myself time each morning to meditate and read, it allows me to remember what makes me happy, what I want to achieve with my business, and the kind of person I want to be when I am with a client, my partner, a friend and even a stranger. My day is then so much more productive, calmer and enjoyable.

I have also found that 'switching off' an hour before bed time is incredibly effectively for a good night's sleep and I wake feeling refreshed, full of energy and feel incredibly calm towards all those challenges I face while running my business. I switch off all technology (pc, phone, TV) and read a book, or sit down with my partner and chat about random things or get confused trying to understand quantum physics!

It is incredible how much more focused, productive and effective I am at achieving my business goals and getting through my workload when I just give myself this time every day, morning and night. Some may think this is a lot especially if your day is filled with working on your business, keeping on top of the housework, cooking the dinner and taking care of your partner, kids, pets, and/or other family members. Yet, giving yourself an hour at the start and end of a day gives your day more productivity. I challenge you to give it a go.

I know your business is probably something you enjoy doing, and you love taking care of your families and/or friends but with all intent and purposes you can likely get caught up in all the drama and excitement and forget about just you. Be fair and give yourself valuable time each day. After all, without you, your business would not exist.

Do you feel guilty about doing something you enjoy?

I love numbers, systems, procedures, organising, reading and writing, but I always struggled accepting this. I was different to many of my friends, and I didn't fit in with many of my fellow accountants. I preferred a more holistic approach to how an organisation operated and wanted to know more about the people behind a business. Slowly over the years I came to realise that I enjoyed doing something that many people didn't feel comfortable doing, and that I had a gift of being able to explain this a lot easier to people and in a down to earth way. This was why I set up in business; to help small businesses with something they dreaded or didn't understand.

Something was not quite right with it though. I was helping lots of small businesses and I felt good about that but there would be days, weeks even, when I would be quite stressed about it all. I knew my stress was the result of the pressure I was putting on myself, but I couldn't understand why.

Gradually it came to light that I was feeling guilty about doing something that came so naturally to me, and therefore I was putting extra pressure on myself. I was giving myself extra work in a day to make myself feel like I had done a hard day's work. Pretty weird huh? However somehow I don't think I am alone!

Stress is also a result of not trusting in life and/or not trusting your decisions. Do you believe it will all be ok? If you align your heart mind with your money mind, and your body and soul minds, then I believe it will be ok. In fact, I know it will be ok.

There are a lot of people out there who give themselves extra work, bigger challenges or tighter deadlines to make themselves feel like they have earned it. I once had client that was always giving themselves challenges; the next one bigger than the last. They now have a serious illness which they also see as a challenge. Where does it stop?

I still believe that you should push yourself and develop your body and mind to do bigger and better things. However, you should also be aware of your thoughts and acknowledge if you are pushing yourself because you feel guilty for having an 'easy life'. I know I certainly was.

Life can be very challenging, and running a business is not for the faint hearted so why give yourself extra pressure? I now acknowledge that my skills are a gift, along with everyone else's out there, which I intend sharing with everyone, and allow myself to enjoy it.

Life will give me challenges I am sure of that, my business will most certainly give me lots, particularly with the constant changes in legislation and tax, therefore I am going to feel a lot more grateful for the days that do feel like a walk in the park and reserve my energy for the real challenges.

Top takeaway from this chapter:

Do you see yourself as the most important person in your life and your business? Do you feel guilty when your life is easy?

PART 4

Do you act in accordance to your success or are you afraid?

TAKING ACTION

In **part one** I talked about making friends with the money mind. Then in **part two** I defined what success would mean for you. In **part three** I asked you to consider that you are worthy of success by listening to your body and your soul. **Part four** will look at what stops you. Once you have aligned all four minds and they are all talking to each other, I will ask what is preventing you from taking action.

Magical things happen but only when you take action

You may be familiar with the law of attraction (focus on what you want and it will come to you) and I do believe magical things happen, however, I also believe you must show the world that you are prepared to help yourselves too. Your success will not come to you by sitting on the side-line waiting. You must take action. You must show the world that you are prepared to reach for your dreams and that involves paying attention to your mindset and what actions you are taking, or not taking.

If you're a therapist or a coach, you're likely more eager to help someone who is helping themselves. If someone is not prepared to venture outside their comfort zone by thinking and/or doing something different then you're not able to help them live to their full potential. I believe life is like this too. It's sending us opportunities every moment of every day.

If you want to do something about the state of your finances, your business and/or your life you will need to take some action. This book can help you with that but you must have the courage to get curious about your own thoughts, your beliefs and behaviours.

It is all about the mindset

I believe that running a business is very similar to disciplining yourself to achieve any goal; whether that is to lose weight, run a marathon, or write a book. You start off with the intention in mind and then plan. Anyone who has been successful in losing weight, an athlete, or an author will tell you, the training and the planning is just a small part of the achievement. The rest is the quality of your mindset and taking action to achieve your goal.

My partner and I enjoy hill-walking and very often we set out with the mountain in full view and start walking full of enthusiasm. At first the path is relatively easy and fun. I soon encounter a steep climb but it is do-able if I focus on what I am doing. On the really steep climbs there comes a point when I feel exhausted. I feel I cannot go on any further, especially if it's our first hill walk after a long winter. In fact, I sometimes question what on earth made me think that this was a good idea before warming up!

This is when I have a choice to make. I can either turnaround and walk back down, or I can choose to hang in there, take a rest, and only move again when I feel the energy has returned to start walking again. There is no right or wrong choice. It's only me that is putting the pressure on myself when I say I must get to the top; *'I'll be a failure if I don't make it'.*

If I focus on feeling tired or how horrible the weather is then I will make my journey that little bit more challenging. If I do decide to start walking back, I will still have learnt what I am capable of and what I need to do if I were to try again. However, if I can find the energy and the right frame of mind to hang in there and keep going at a steady pace, when I reach the top it feels incredible to know that I persevered and I know I have learnt a little more about myself along the way.

In business, some days reaching the top can just be all about getting to the end of the day without being stressed and reaching for the alcohol! If you are lucky though, you can look back on the day, the week, month or even year and see things differently.

High up on the mountain top I see things I've never seen before, and experience moments that I've learnt from. I understand more about what is around me and how many others are climbing too. I see my business being very similar to this. I have met so many people through my work, most of whom are now my friends, and I have learnt about things I didn't know even existed.

I'd been helping businesses for many years as a management accountant (an accountant that reports on and helps businesses with their performance) yet admittedly, it wasn't until I ran by own business as a finance coach before I understood just how challenging it was!

I was familiar with how much our mindset influences our behaviour but I never realised just how much it stopped us from doing things. You can be really skilled in what you do and have a great team behind you (and that team can be your family and friends for most self-employed business owners) but the energy and the choices can only come from you. That is where having the right mindset then taking action is crucial.

Top takeaway from this chapter:

It is challenging and scary running a business but life doesn't stand still for us. If you don't flex your muscles every now and again you get comfortable and then you will be unable to move when you need to. If you exercise your fear muscles regularly, even in small doses, then you will prepare yourself for a successful business and a successful life.

ARE YOU BEHAVING IN ACCORDANCE TO SUCCESS?

Are you truly aligned with success or are self-sabotaging it?

If you wanted to lose weight, would you consider walking somewhere instead of getting the bus and eating a little less? Alternatively, would you still continue to get the bus/car everywhere and reach into the fridge or cupboards between meal times?

Hopefully you said yes to the first scenario!

If I asked you to apply the same discipline with your business, what behaviours are appropriate to your success?

Take out what you noted down in part two for your intentions and make any changes after what you read in part three, if you have not already done so. Now think what kind of behaviours would be needed for these intentions to materialise. Think of at least three of each intention. Yes, three! That way if one of them can't be done, you still have another two to fall back on.

Do your intentions include financial freedom in order to go travelling in five years' time or is it the flexibility to spend more time with your family?

If it is either of these, then spending money now, instead of saving it, will not get you there. This is an example of our actions not being aligned with our success.

As I explained in part three, you have to think of the reasons why you are buying something each time. Is it because you feel like you deserve it, and I am sure you do! Ask yourself if there are other ways you could treat yourself that would allow you to save more now so you achieve success sooner.

I really do encourage you to look at why you buy things. Look at what feelings you are craving and consider how your behaviour could contribute to that. Explore what it is that you really crave. This will help with part two too.

You may not have financial freedom just yet or full-blown success but you do have freedom to choose what you do today and what you buy today.

Are you choosing success today or are you delaying it?

If you want to spend time with your family/friends, read a book, or do two hours of yoga each day, then you can choose to do that now. As I said in part two, make your business work around the lifestyle you want.

When you run your own business you have so much more freedom than if you were employed. No-one makes you work certain hours other than connecting with your customers. You can work the hours that suit you. You then just have to adjust your price and business model accordingly.

If you have children, then it's likely that you'll want to work around their school times and doing the housework. Yet I wonder if you're ok with that. One of my clients felt she had to put in at least forty-eight hours a week, so she was working in the evenings when the kids were in bed. That worked whilst they were younger but now that they are older and going to bed later, Laura was having to work later into the night. She now knows she has to work efficiently on one thing that matters to her and gives her a profit in addition to time with her family.

Hopefully by now you will be aware of what beliefs you have had running in the background that may have been blocking your chances of more money and a successful business. However, if you are still not getting the results you want then you may need to dig a little deeper. The great thing about being mindful of your thoughts and actions is that you start to have a relationship with your subconscious.

Top takeaway from this chapter:

Are you contributing every day to your success or are you self-sabotaging it? If so, why?

WHAT UNCONSCIOUS PROGRAMS DO YOU NEED TO UPDATE?

When you first get a new computer or smartphone you install it with programs and apps. Then each time you start them up you have everything all ready for you. The computer and your smartphone are programmed with what you need and they are designed to check for updates regularly. You never need to bother about it again until they start to get slow or old or just stop working.

Your subconscious is where your programs (beliefs and habits) were installed years ago. It carries out the same routines and beliefs on autopilot. It does stuff without you having to think about it. When you set an intention or something reminds you about a similar experience, you are asking your subconscious to run a specific program and it does. No questions asked, just like a computer program. The difference is that computer programs automatically update. Our subconscious does not.

You therefore need to manually check your programs for updates. You need to consider if a certain behaviour or belief that was once installed is still serving you. For example, if you used to believe money was about being greedy but now you understand it to be about loving your business, loving others and loving yourself, you need to update that old program. That requires listing all the reasons why the new beliefs are better and then adopting new behaviours that align with that.

Problems can arise when you are not aware of what program was installed to make you feel the way you do, or why you do certain things, such as sabotaging your success. Additionally, you may be aware of what is stopping you but find it challenging to change your old behaviours and beliefs.

There is hope though. Hypnotherapists and psychologists, amongst other professionals, can work with your subconscious on a behaviour without you ever knowing what the program was. For example, some people work with a hypnotherapist to stop smoking. Often they don't remember why they started smoking but they know they want to stop. The hypnotherapist leads them into a nice relaxed state (also known as trance) and reminds them of all the reasons why they want to stop. The reason behind the relaxed state is so that the individual gets access to what their heart, body and soul want as well as what the head wants. Additionally, the majority of unwanted behaviours are the result of stress and once an individual experiences a relaxed state and is taught how to return there, this can really help to kick the bad habits.

This type of therapy can be successful for most people, but there are a few occasions when it doesn't work. This could be for many reasons. Whether someone truly wanted the change is one crucial success factor, but it is possibly because the individual has not learned how to adapt in their old environment without the behaviour they have always been used to doing. Maybe it's because the program that installed the behaviour was very powerful for them, or there's one program that is interfering with another. This then requires being more mindful about their feelings and thoughts.

Some people say affirmations and mantras, in addition to doing tapping/EFT (Emotional Freedom Technique) to get over their blocks about money and some of these can be incredibly useful. However, if you have tried some or all of these and only noticed a slight shift then it's very likely that there's another program that's still sitting in your subconscious which needs updated. It may or not be directly linked with money or success but it's definitely something that's stopping you.

Being incredibly mindful and questioning everything you are doing will help you to identify it. Some questions below are useful but please seek out a coach or therapist if you have any reason to believe that it's linked to a traumatic experience.

- What did I gain from that behaviour just there?
- What feeling triggered that behaviour?
- Am I avoiding feeling something? Why?
- What was I thinking before I did x, felt y or said z?
- Have I ever felt this before at all? If yes, when was the first time I felt this?
- What happened and how did I cope with that?

How two or more programs can interfere with each other and cause a meltdown

To give you an idea of the programs you can download as a result of our younger experiences, and how complex they can get, I'm going to share more of my story.

In part one I told you about my intention, aged ten, to be financially independent after being annoyed at my mum for being dependent on my violent alcoholic father for money. This was a program that benefited me well throughout the best part of my life yet it also caused me to have a meltdown. It drove me to push myself to the extreme. Anytime I didn't feel happy my subconscious thought oh she needs to be working hard and earning more money because that will make her happy. That was the program I installed. However, it didn't stop to ask; will that action always fulfil the goal of happiness?

This program had me working every weekend and holidays from primary six to just a few years ago. I still find myself working seven days a week but only when I have a project that requires it and then I ensure I have a few days off shortly after.

Because of my financial goal I was very good at managing money. However, I soon found myself in debt with student loans after I left University. My first full time job was poorly paid and I put my professional accountancy training on my credit card. I was not comfortable with debt but I saw it as investing in my future so I accepted it. I soon got too friendly with the credit card though and would use it for other things like new clothes every time I was going out somewhere with friends and I would also take cash out with the credit card too to pay for these nights out (please never do this!).

Why was I doing this when I wanted to be financially independent?

Interestingly, it was because I had downloaded another program to my subconscious. That program was that I am not loved and never good enough ie I had a lack of self-love. This is why I recognise it in so many of my clients.

When I met my current partner, who was completely debt free including his student loans, it was a stark reminder for me of how badly I had allowed my relationship with money to get. Because I was feeling loved (I was in a great relationship), I renewed my vow to myself (and if honest also wanting to impress my new boyfriend!) and made a conscious decision to repay my loans as quickly as I could.

We were both open about money in our relationship, which I highly recommend, and our holidays were only day trips when we could afford the petrol or the odd camping holiday when we had a bit more money to spare. There was one camping holiday up in the north west of Scotland during very stormy weather that reinforced my desire for money. The trip up to Skye was not particularly pleasant. It was lashing rain and gales of up to 45mph, and the first campsite we came to had a hotel opposite that I really wished we were in! We had to go into the hotel to pay for our pitch, so I enquired into the price of a room for the night. It was ten times the price of the pitch and I knew the only way I could pay for it was to use the credit card that I'd recently cut up! That night my determination to pay off my debts and afford the luxury of a dry and warm room was higher than ever. In my opinion, anyone that says money cannot buy happiness has not camped out in stormy night and be teased by the inviting warmth of a hotel staring back them!

It was incredibly challenging but I did pay off all my loans including my student loan and built up savings which I owe to my determination (and camping out in that wet stormy night). Napoleon Hill spoke about desire being one of the strongest motivators in our life, and our business, to get anything done and based on my experience I would agree!

However I soon forgot. I mentioned in part two that when I left employment to run my business full-time I ignored my money mind. I did this because I had ignored my heart, body and soul and had downloaded another program that said happiness can only be achieved by ignoring the money mind. I was physically exhausted and very unhappy with my life and so I thought if I wanted to be happy I had to choose between my head and my heart. I choose heart. Yet I had no money (savings aside) and I had to take my partner shopping with me when he was free at the weekend to get a pair of jeans. Suddenly I realised I was dependent on my partner who had started to get a little frustrated that I was not earning as much as I used to. I was really not happy about that either, but I was also confused. I had one program saying ignore the money mind, another telling me strive for financial independence, and another feeling unloved!

It was in this moment of upset and frustration I applied for a job, as I mentioned earlier. During the interview though I realised it was not what I wanted. I walked out the interview with a renewed sense of determination of wanting my business to work. I talked myself into pretending everything was ok. I told myself it was a sacrifice I had to make to build my business - however I was still ignoring my bank balance. This was against everything I believed in. I was telling everyone to always keep an eye on their finances and here I was most definitely not practicing what I preached. Like everyone else who does not have enough money I didn't want to be reminded of my lack of funds constantly and so I ignored them. It was incongruent to who I was as an accountant (this is why being authentic is essential) and

I knew deep down it was definitely not the best strategy! However, the turning point was when I was out with friends for dinner.

There was eight of us having a Christmas meal together. I had £30 on me so I restricted myself to what I ate despite most of my friends having three courses plus a few glasses of wine. When it came to paying the bill it was suggested that we just split the bill which came to £50 each.

I know now that I should have spoken up and my friends would have understood, but I was so embarrassed about not having enough money so I kept quite whilst wondering what the heck I was going to do. Thankfully I was incredible fortunate enough to have a very intuitive friend in the group. Oblivious to the others she thrust a £20 note into my hand under the table. I was gobsmacked at her generosity, and her intuition. It was also a little heart wrenching too as I remembered that she had told me a few months earlier, money was a bit tight for her. I made my way to the ladies toilet to hide the tears. She followed me and asked if it was enough and did I need more, at which point the flood gates opened.

That night as I drove home I realised I needed to find the courage to always be honest about my money, be authentic about having a passion for money and align my actions with my values. I also needed to stop the negative patterns in my life and be mindful about my behaviour. I had to become conscious of what was going on and really get to work with the unconscious conflicting beliefs I had.

The next day I went through my partner and I's finances working out where more savings could be made but equally looking at what I needed to be making in my business in order to contribute to the household. I made more of a conscious effort to say yes to opportunities even if they were outside my comfort zone but more importantly I vowed to be authentic and tell the truth to everyone.

When I was honest to other business owners that starting a business was a financial struggle for me and I was finding it tough, I was surprised when so many people agreed with me. This was interesting to experience as most of them had told others that their business was going well. Yet, when approached on a more intimate level they admitted the truth too.

When I started looking at my beliefs and behaviours, I found it upsetting. I had blamed a lot of people for my situation, particularly my father. However, once I realised the last fifteen years of my life were all my own doing (and my father had been dead for eight years) the realisation hit me. It was not pleasant to realise that I was at fault for the thoughts, actions and behaviours in my life which I'd blamed others for. Yet, the more authentic I became, the more compassion I had for my younger self and even my father (more of that in another book!). The deeper I probed into my unconscious the more pleasant my surroundings became.

I'm now often at the right place at the right time. I get new clients and am invited to be part of new projects, or just have the right people come along when I need them. I'm now curious and honest about everything in my life regardless of how I believe others may judge me.

I constantly question my behaviours and beliefs and I am thankfully surrounded by fellow coaches, hypnotherapists and trainee psychologists all whom I can call on to help me work through something if I am getting stuck myself. I also find the more authentic I am; the more authentic others are around me too. The only time I feel that life is against me is when I am not taking responsibility for my actions and blaming others.

I believe life is like our own personal coach. It sees you making an effort and then gives you a helping hand. However, if it sees you blaming everyone and not being accountable for your thoughts, feelings and actions then it will do something that nudges you to realign.

As I mentioned in part one, on an energetic level, life will give us what we send out. If you sent out thoughts of wanting to help others and be successful then that is what you will get. If you send out thoughts of blame and negativity, then that is what you will attract more of in your life. If you are unfamiliar with this stuff, then I recommend some great books in the index, but do your own life experiments. I do them all the time but the important thing to remember is to ask for what you want. Even if that is just guidance.

I recently felt a bit overwhelmed with the editing of this book in addition to my psychology studies starting back up, and business as normal. I had scheduled to go to a new networking event and quite honestly I couldn't be bothered. After my morning meditation I felt more energised with a sense of just go and see what happens. I did. After we had all introduced ourselves a lady came up to me and said *"You are never going to believe this, but I asked the universe this morning for a finance coach and when you introduced yourself I nearly fell over!"* This was all the evidence I needed to show me that life will guide me and support me in my endeavours. Please do your own experiments if you don't believe me but remember to keep an open mind!

Moments like this can also be described as coincidences although the psychologist Carl Jung, explained these as Synchronicities; a principle which explains collective unconscious. What you believe will determine how you view coincidences and everyone is entitled to their own opinion. I trust that there is something far bigger and far more powerful out there than we can possibly imagine. That can be God for some people, or it can be spirit, or source, or consciousness itself, or maybe it is something else for you. All I encourage you to do is keep an open mind and believe anything is possible whilst conducting your own experiments.

Top takeaway from this chapter:

When things are not going well in our life or
business it is often the result of old programs.
You are responsible for your own happiness,
for your own success.

I love the following quote from a friend of mine
*"Depression, anxiety, anger, stress – all these feelings
are simply an absence of the positive. These aren't
necessary an illness and you definitely aren't broken
beyond repair... Your mind is giving you a hard kick
up the arse and looking for you to make decision!!"*
– Breakthrough: A blueprint for your mind
by Brian Costello (page 138).

HAVE FAITH AND TAKE ACTION

Nothing gets done by just dreaming about it. You need to take a step forward and look where you're going.

Successful business owners don't worry about the finer details of how they will achieve their goal. They use the information their business, and their own mind, tells them to guide them and make adjustments as they take each step forward. These include their finances, sales figures, customer feedback, and as mentioned in the last chapter, how they feel.

Think of it like walking down a busy main street to reach a shop on the opposite side of the road. You don't doubt for one second that you will not make it, nor do you know exactly, step by step, how you are going to get there although you have a fairly good idea. You start walking by paying attention to where you are stepping. You then wait at the pedestrian crossing for the traffic lights to change, so you can cross the road. You will walk around bus stops, lamp posts or a crowd of people on the pavement. Eventually you will reach the shop. You simply manoeuvred your way around. However, if you were to have your eyes shut, the chances are that you would either bump into someone on the pavement, or get hit by a car crossing the road!

Every day in your business you are walking down that busy street. Your goal is tuning into your passion and getting your service/products out to everyone who needs them. You may not be exactly sure how this will happen in fine detail, but to move forwards successfully in your business, your eyes need to be open. You can then take a step forward and interact with your environment, whilst your mind is calculating any adjustments that need to be made.

Your eyes need to focus on where you're going but equally scanning the immediate environment for feedback. By reviewing your finances and other targets this tells you what adjustments, if any, need to be made. This is where your mini intentions are useful (remember the chapter 'How will you recognise success?). They keep you focussed on what you want.

Remember to be compassionate on your journey though, as you will sometimes have to take a side step to pause for a moment, or to avoid an obstacle coming towards you. That is ok. Acknowledge why you need to take those actions by understanding the obstacle. These obstacles are opportunities in disguise, because every obstacle that comes your way will have something to teach you. Your thoughts, beliefs, actions and finances will all tell you the answers you need to hear. This is why it is essential to pay attention to things like lack of sales, no money or feeling down because they will all tell you ensure your head, heart, body and soul are aligned before taking action.

Top takeaway from this chapter:

Trust that you will be guided each and every step if you pay attention to your head, heart, body and soul. Scan your environment, look at your accounts, sales and other business related information and take action.

IS FEAR HOLDING YOU BACK?

"Fear: False Expectations Appearing Real" – Susan Jeffers

Fear is an interesting concept. It can protect you if you are thinking of doing something that will kill you, yet fear also stops you from doing so many things that would never harm you.

During the third year of my business I took a leap of faith to grow my business by employing a full time member of staff, whilst moving out of my home office and into a serviced office nearby. I did a cashflow and profit forecast and knew everything would be ok for the first three months. I was not sure what would happen after that but both my assistant and I were prepared to just wait and see as the weeks unfolded.

I sourced and applied for funding from the local government to help me with some of the costs and thankfully I had savings too. I also had the systems in place to assess what my sales and profit were on a monthly basis, so I could tell mid-month if it was looking good or if some changes needed to be made. I spoke with a couple of business owners who had expressed interest in working with me, and met with my existing clients and told them they may get someone else when they called me. I was entering new ground and it was very scary but equally I knew it was what I wanted. My heart wanted me to write books and do more 1-1 work. I could only make this happen by making a few adjustments and taking a few scary decisions.

I got a few things wrong, but I got a few things right too! The things I did wrong I put them down to experience and can tell my clients who are growing a business so they do the right things, and I gave myself a pat on the back for the things I did right. I'm glad I did it though and I really encourage you to take a leap of faith.

What actually is fear?

Fear is a personal perception that can stop you from achieving your business goals. It is an emotional response to what you perceive is danger. You need it to survive, or you would constantly be putting your life in danger. However, you can also feel fear when you are scared to do something different, or when you are feeling nervous about going beyond your comfort zone. It is important that we know the difference between these two types of fears.

Fear helped your ancestors to survive and it was because of their fear that you are born. They had to fear predators in order to ensure their survival. They would hear a rustle in the bush and run. Sometimes it was a predator, sometimes it was not but they couldn't hang around to find out or they would be dead. That kind of perceived fear is good. The other type of fear that has you running for no reason is a waste of time and energy.

When you feel a little scared, question what it is that you are scared of. Are you perhaps a little bit uncomfortable about something that is forcing you to change the way you do business; encouraging you to do something different? Alternatively, are you imagining something that's not yet happened, but you perceive might happen?

If it has not happened, then the perceived outcome is what you can imagine in that moment based on experiences and old programmed beliefs. Explore if you can make that ending better, just like you would if you were telling a child a story.

A lot of your anxiety comes from resisting change, avoiding challenges, and fearing something that is just imagined. It is important that you don't allow your fears to jeopardise your ambitions. If you once dreamed of something great for your business, it can still happen. It may be tough, but rise to the challenges and don't let fear hold you back.

Jane, a client, was fearing taking action in her business. When we discussed previous occasions that she had initially feared, she acknowledged that the outcome was never as worse than she had thought. Based on my own experience, I had to agree.

Fear really is an illusion

When my partner and I first allowed our adopted four-year-old cat outside after her two-week incubation period, she jumped up on to the roof of our house. Thankfully we live in a bungalow so it was not too high a drop, but nonetheless it was not somewhere I would choose to venture. This was the same cat that had run and hidden from the vacuum cleaner earlier that day!

I was worried about her, yet equally impressed after I soon realised that the fear of her being up there was mine, not hers. I turned my back (partly because I couldn't look!) and hoped she would come safely back down. She did.

She got me thinking about parachute jumpers, rock climbers, divers, and people who like spiders. How is it that some people are fearful of a situation yet to someone else there is nothing wrong with it, in fact they go as far as loving it?

When I fear something that others have no problem with, it reminds me that my perception of what could happen differs from them, and what I think, is just imagined. In those moments I now see encouragement to try something that I would have previously shied away from.

I am not recommending you climb up on your house roof like my cat, or jump out off a plane (although I hear it is good fun) unless you want to! Although, I do feel many business owners hold back from developing their business further for fear of something. You may fear being truly successful or making a big mistake yet others don't let these things hold them back. What if you questioned your fears a little closely, and asked what you're really scared of and answer the following question: Is it an illusion or real?

Do you fear failing?

One of the biggest fears mostly everyone has is the fear of failing. When coaches, inspirational speakers and positive minded individuals ask you to think of the best positive outcome, no-one is telling you to let go of reality. What you are being asked to do is question the perception of your reality that is forming in your imagination.

Is it really true? And so what if you fail?

According to the Collins English dictionary failing means to *"be unsuccessful in an undertaking"* yet it also describes it as *"neglect to do something"*. It is obviously just a matter of which explanation you wish to focus on.

To me, failure is simply not trying. Thomas Edison, the man who invented the light bulb, was reported to have said that he never believed he failed. He only ever just ruled out another way not to do something. I don't know if he really said that, but nonetheless I like that mindset.

I have made many mistakes in my life yet they have all shaped me, and I am able to share my experiences with my clients and to you through my books, and let's be honest, something is only ever wrong in hindsight!

Whenever you do something you are only ever taking that step forward with the knowledge you have at the time. It is really only ever just feedback, never failure. That is why it is important to step forward with your eyes open so you can see and feel that feedback then make corrections if necessary. This is what everyone should be doing.

Maybe we're on this planet for a reason or maybe we're not. Maybe our lives are just pure chance. Regardless of what you believe, we're all just trying to do the best we can.

Are you avoiding disappointment?

Most people believe that if they don't do something then they cannot be disappointed. I believe you will be more disappointed with the things you didn't do than the things you did. My personal experience certainly tells me that! I'm disappointed with myself for not overcoming my fears when younger and doing what I really wanted to do.

Nothing is real until it happens, or it is proven a scientific certainty, although that can even still be challenged! All science does is prove (or disprove) a theory with the evidence available at any given moment in time.

When something happens that disappoints you, remember that although it didn't give you the results you were hoping for, it did give you an experience to talk about and learn from.

I was talking to a client about this recently. We usually imagine the worst, and most times the worst doesn't happen but on very rare occasions, the worst can happen. The reason is because of what you are focusing on. When you focus on where you don't want to go, that is where you go! (Remember the motorbike example in the chapter 'What do you really want?) This doesn't mean that you should be in denial over a possible outcome but you should be concentrating all your efforts on what you want to happen.

For example, another client of mine foresaw their two biggest customers significantly reducing the revenue they gave them. The worst outcome was that this did happen, the best outcome was that nothing changed. If ABC Ltd had remained positive, they would not have been worried at all and assumed no change. However, in reality they knew, given the circumstances, that this was extremely unlikely. So they concentrated their efforts on other opportunities, whilst they spoke with their two biggest customers. It turned out there was a dip in sales from them. This would have meant job losses if ABC Ltd had not feared it and taken action. However, because they took action and explored new opportunities they found themselves in a position of having to employ more staff to cope with demand!

Most things can only be learnt by doing them

Sometimes though, we just have to go ahead and make mistakes!

I was looking after my godson aged three, one afternoon. During our playtime, I became aware of saying 'be careful' about ten times in five minutes. We were playing with paints and water and I was a worried that he would spill water on the floor or get paint on the kitchen table or his top. I soon realised though, that each of those outcomes were harmless and could easily be cleaned up. However, what was more important was how was he ever going to learn if he didn't see what his actions could do, for himself? I then relaxed and let him do what he wanted, and started having fun myself. I stood back and observed when he walked across the house with a full cup of water.

He spilt a little water on one journey across the house and he immediate said "Oops too much water" and filled up with a little less the next time. He got some paint on the table and again it was 'oops' and this time he asked for a cloth. He then moved to the sink and plugged the drain with the tap on full. I sat watching as the water got dangerously close to the rim, then milliseconds before I jumped in to turn the tap off and unplug the drain, I saw his eyes register what was going on. He then reached across and turned the tap off himself again with an 'oops' followed by a giggle.

Sometimes kids, and adults, do get it wrong, but how else can they learn? You have to try things to know how close you can actually get to the edge, and how much fun it can be.

Top takeaway from this chapter:

None of us want to be disappointed but if we don't go after new opportunities or make mistakes we are never going to learn anything new. Bring in compassion to past mistakes and be curious just like a child again.

BE OPEN TO NEW EXPERIENCES

Alisoun Mackenzie shared with me that she believed we must do something that we enjoy in our business and keep an open mind about the paths our heart leads us. The reason being because sometimes we just don't know what fabulous places they will take us.

This really resonated with me, as I'm a firm believer in both of those statements. Opportunities can come along when you least expect them and you will often have no idea where they will take you. If it feels right and it's something you love and enjoy, then you are almost guaranteed that it will be a path that will lead you to something amazing. It may even take you somewhere you had no intention of going but yet you will gain the same results that you were dreaming of. This is why you must let go of the detail and only focus on what you want to achieve: the end results; how you want to feel.

I mentioned earlier that I was scared at my lack of money and went for a job interview. I could have looked at that as failure but during the interview I got on well with one of the guys on the interview panel. I walked out there knowing I didn't want the job but I knew something would come from the experience. I didn't know what but something told me it would, and it did.

Within a couple of months of the interview I got a call from the recruitment agency asking me if they could pass my details on to one of the guys on the interview panel. I said yes of course! It turned out he knew a company who was looking for some consultancy work and would I be interested. The opportunity turned out to be a very big client for me for a while, and they introduced me to another couple of big clients. If I had not gone for that interview, I believe I would not have got those opportunities. Trust your 'failures'. They might just be your biggest savior.

Look for the possibilities

When you were a child you thought anything was possible. You believed a man in a red suit was able to deliver presents to everyone in the world on Christmas Eve with the aid of twelve flying reindeers and enter everyone's homes via their chimneys. There were no limitations, no doubts and no 'but what if's'.

Ok, so it is a story but sadly most people look at everything now with a filtered opinion. They look at it with the knowledge of their previous experiences and/or with information they have gained from others, in addition to mindset of everything is impossible.

It is common to look at current and new opportunities based on past experiences but if you want to be successful, you must look at opportunities for your business with an open mind. You must not attach the old experiences to them. Certainly learn from your experiences but that doesn't mean that you should dismiss all similar prospects.

When you go out for dinner and have a bad meal, I assume you don't go back to that restaurant again until there is a new chef and/or a change of management. Yet I would bet that does not stop you from going out to another restaurant and having the same meal eg Chicken Curry.

Be open minded with all opportunities that come along. Stop dismissing opportunities based solely on previous experiences. The world has changed since then and so have you.

"Our greatest weakness lies in giving up. The most certain way to succeed is to try just one more time" - Thomas A Edison

Stop Waiting

If it is not fear but the possibility that you are waiting for encouragement from someone or something in your life, then stop. Stop waiting on someone to give you that helping hand. So often I hear of people not taking their business to that next step because they are waiting on a lottery win, a big project from a customer, or funding from the bank/government.

If this is you then I have three words for you - in the words of Nike famous 1980's slogan - 'Just Do It'. You could even download an image from the internet and print out or put on your desktop. Trust me, it works!

As a finance coach I would advise that you work out how much you need before you start so you can be focussed on achieving it and ensure it is realistic. This is why you need to listen to your money mind as well as your heart. However, you can still take steps towards it, take it up a gear. Often the more challenged you are to find the funds to grow, the more you do actually grow because you take those steps outside our comfort zone.

Before I started my business full time I was unhappily waiting for a lottery win or my partner to insist that I left my job. Neither were forthcoming, so one day I sat down and worked out if we could afford to live on my partner's wage for a few months. After I identified what luxuries we could cut (mostly all mine which I felt was fair!), and calculated that we could live on his wage, I then discussed my plans with him. He was impressed I had done my calculations first and had all the answers for him. He agreed too!

Listen to the frustrations that your emotions are telling you and take a leap of faith. I have learned a lot, and have made a few mistakes, but if I were to go back, I would still choose to do most of them!

Are you trusting life or holding back?

So many times in my life I have noticed that when I don't trust the events that are unfolding in my life, or a certain person I have come across, I am often on the receiving end of someone not trusting me. This is why acknowledging your thoughts through practises such as mindfulness and meditation can be useful, as they allow you to explore what you are thinking. You will have noticed that I encourage you throughout this book to become a scientist and do some experiments.

Writing or meditating are also important too. A lot of my clients meditate regularly, and find that journaling either after their meditation practice, or instead of, can also be quite effective. Some of my clients even bring their journals to our sessions where we review something that came up for them.

I certainly notice that when I write down the reasons why I am upset or frustrated at something, I get clarity on the challenge.

I ask myself a series of questions which I will share with my clients and I will with you too:

1. Am I trusting life? If not, why not?
2. Am I following my joy? If not, why not?
3. Am I being fearful of the potential outcome? If yes, why? What I am thinking?
4. If I loved myself would I do, think, or feel, this?

My clients find all of these questions incredibly insightful, particularly the last one, which is why part three of this book was dedicated to it. The quickest shortcut to success is to trust and believe in yourself.

Top takeaway from this chapter:

Believe that something good will come out of any challenge you are experiencing. This does not mean that it is not happening but remaining hopeful will have your 'four minds' looking for solutions. Trust in life and believe the impossible.

ADDICTIONS, SABOTAGE AND PATIENCE

We value the comfort of the short term quick fix more than the long term need. This has been proven by psychology research and experiments.

For example, the comfort of eating a large tasty packet of crisps or a massive delicious slice of cake often prevails over the long term goodness of our health. Having the occasional packet of crisps or a slice of cake is ok for our health but not if we have them every day. When we need this comfort every day it becomes an addiction. Comfort and routine is innate in our behaviour.

Your addictions can sabotage your business though. You will either be motivated to move away from pain or move towards a reward depending on the thing you want and the environment you are in. Find out what works for you and use that as the motivation towards your big goal.

Focus on the thing you DO want and really visualise that each day for a moment. Perhaps as you drift off to sleep. That programs your mind to thinking it's possible. Sometimes when you really don't believe it can happen, perhaps because of habits, you need to then think about the pain and use those negative images to propel you away. (I would recommend working on the positive thoughts though as if you think about the negative ones for long enough you will unconsciously head towards that destination.)

Change involves taking action and that can be challenging, but help is available. Get a finance or business coach to help you through the tough times. They will not do it for you but they will be there to give you some moral support. If you can't afford a coach, then buddy up with another business owner. Choose carefully though as the difference between a coach and a friend is that the coach knows tips and techniques to help you through those challenges. However, a friend could just maybe be there to hold your hand and talk to at 10pm at night. You will be hard pushed to find a coach available to chat to you at that time of night unless they're in a different time zone! Choose a friend that has some knowledge, preferably a coach or therapist who is offering swaps and you have something to give them.

You will need to step outside your comfort zone. Just like when you learned to walk as a toddler, it's all about taking baby steps. That may involve crawling gently for a bit to explore the new experience. Then when you feel confident, you take that first step by holding onto something or someone. When you feel ready to let go, let go. You may fall, you may not, but just like when you fell as a toddler, just get back up and try again.

I didn't ask for support for a long time, but little things in my life reminded me that I needed the support of others. I almost broke my arm on holiday when questioning whether I should get another coach and I was having a tough time at work when I was thinking I was not being supported. Enlisting a coach early on was key for me to grow my business. I stopped working with her for a while to integrate the learnings and then I enlisted the help of another coach when I was ready to move forward and felt I needed support again.

If you feel things are challenging I really do encourage you to speak up and ask for help. That could be just talking to your partner or kids about helping round the house, or like me recently buying a dishwasher! It could be arranging to have regular meet ups with an encouraging friend or swaps with a coach or actually enlisting the services of a professional coach. Choose what suits your business, your finances and the help you need right now.

Whatever you do, speak to someone. Equally be prepared for them to only give advice. They cannot do it for you. When it comes to selling your business and growing your business that has to come from you. Alternatively, you can delegate tasks by employing an assistant or a sales person.

Top takeaway from this chapter:

Change is daunting but it is made easier when we are
surrounded by a supporting team and we are
focussed on which direction we want to go and why.
Find you supportive team.

BE PRESENT AND TRUST

"We must let go of the life we had planned so as to expect the life that is waiting for us"
Joseph Campbell.

I encourage you to live in the moment with passion. Have less of an attachment to a detailed outcome and more an involvement in what is happening right now. Be fully present in the moment. Your thoughts create feelings. Low moods, negativity and pain are caused by attachment to thought. Let the thought pass like a cloud in the sky or like a wave in the ocean.

The quality of our mind is the only thing that affects your progress. Take yourself away from the problem by going for a walk or meet up with a friend. You will find a different perspective on it. Do something other than thinking about it. The solution is found in the present moment. It is not found in thinking about the problem.

The answer to all your problems can all be found in your subconscious mind and to reach that place you need to let yourself relax and align your head, heart, body and soul. Often I go to sleep with a challenge in my mind. I am not worried about it but I wonder what options I have. I will write a few ideas down by consciously thinking of the problem. Then I put my pen down and head off to bed or read a book. When I wake I often think off another idea that I can add to the list. More ideas will often come to me when I'm making breakfast or during my morning meditation or out walking too.

They don't always come the next morning after thinking of the challenge. Sometimes it is a day or two later, but they do come to me. The key is to trust that there may be a different solution to the one that your rational mind has come up with.

Each of your four minds; the cognitive mind (head), the emotional mind (heart) and the somatic mind (body) and intuitive mind (soul) will each give valid solutions. The one that is the best one for you is the one that is aligned with all four.

Goal setting

I feel that goals can be taken too seriously and invite stress, but it can also be motivating to have goals. I do prefer to call them intentions. They feel a little more relaxed that way. I feel they still encourage you to get things done but just without the pressure!

Use the following template for your intentions:

- ✓ It must be something that YOU want to accomplish; something that you are excited about and have reasons for wanting it to happen. You must be the driver of these intentions, not your partner, family or friends. They are your intentions and they must be what YOU want.
- ✓ Write down why you want to achieve your intentions as you will refer to this list many times on the tough days for motivation. Be creative too if you want and have some pictures or images that will help inspire you.

- ✓ Write them in the present tense, as if you have accomplished them and you are declaring your achievements. This helps your brain recognise that the task is achievable and almost fools it into thinking that it has achieved it before and can do so again.
- ✓ Have a flexible completion date. Work towards it but if something comes up, bring compassion to the intention.

The next step is to build the framework for each of your intentions. I find it useful to work backwards, giving yourself mini-intentions with various steps you would need to climb to contribute to each of them. Mini-intentions are really the steps that are needed to accomplish your master goal. When you break down your intentions into many manageable chunks the task does not appear so overwhelming. It can also serve as a reward particularly if it could take several months to achieve your main goal.

Example – launching a new product/service.

A typical intention would be to launch a new product or service. The next step would be to look at all the things needed to achieve this. These would then be your mini-intentions and some examples would be carrying out product research, customer research, competitor analysis, sourcing funding, and advertising your business. Each of these would need to be broken into secondary mini-intentions to make the tasks more manageable and giving you a better indication of where to start. For example, when looking at the mini-intention of advertising your business, you would then have to think about things like a website, any social media sites you would want to be on, your name and logo, how you would reach your potential customers, etc.

Review and remind yourself of your intentions regularly

When working towards a very big intention, you may start to question why you are doing it especially if it is taking several months to achieve, or longer! That's perfectly normal. You should always be reviewing your intentions and reminding yourself why you are working towards them. If it's challenging and getting you down remind yourself, why you wanted to do it in the first instance.

Give your intention power. List all the reasons why you want this, then list all the things that would happen if you don't do this. You should find that this exercise will give you some added strength. If something is too hard and you feel that you lack the skills to do it, then that is ok too. Review if it can be done by someone else, or get some training if it's a skill set that you wish to have. Additionally, ask people that you know who have accomplished similar intentions and question how they got over this hurdle. For example, I enlisted the help of a book mentor specifically to help me launch my books.

Be open to adapting your intentions

It is important to be flexible and have an open mind to adjust your intentions slightly if something no longer motivates you, or inspires you, especially if something major in your life has changed, or the intention was determined a few years ago. That's ok but it's important to only adjust your intention because it no longer excites you, and not because it's hard work. This will only frustrate you at a later date for giving up.

If you walk away from your intention because it requires a little effort on your behalf, then you will find that this will happen with a lot of things in life. However, it is equally important not to be hard on yourself. There is enough stress in our daily lives without adding the pressure of a target that only you have set yourself. Life is constantly challenging you with situations such as your partner/parents/kids/pets getting sick, accidents such as losing all your research work, the money saved is needed for an emergency, etc. Be open to having a moveable completion date and be open to changing the fine detail of the intention.

Identify if it is just motivation that challenges you, in which case a good motivational booster when it is getting tough is to visualise yourself having accomplished the intention and imagine what you think it would feel like to have achieved it. Stay with that feeling for a while and then go back and add to your list of reasons why you want this intention. You should find that you have more enthusiasm for it and more reasons to do it. I have an audio link available in part five to download that will help you with this.

Top takeaway from this chapter:

Each of your four minds; the logical mind (head), the emotional mind (heart) and the somatic mind (body) and intuitive mind (soul) will each give valid solutions to your problems. Listen to them and choose the one that is aligned with all four. List your intentions and check in with them every day. On your 'to-do' list, write beside each to do which intention (goal) that will contribute to. Head for your goal but be present and trust in the day to day unfolding of your goal.

BUT HOW DO I BE SOMEONE ELSE

It is likely that another reason you fear doing something or being someone different, is because your beliefs have been your guidelines for all of your life. They are your blueprint. They tell you what to do and they tell you what to be. They determine who you are.

However, did you know that your identity changes over time?

When you are born you are a child, the son or daughter to your parents. When you go to school you become a pupil to your teachers then later a companion to your friends. When you leave school you become a seeker of knowledge and experiences. When you get a job, you become an employee and the role you take on will determine if you are logical, analytical or creative. If you are in a relationship you become a partner, a wife or husband. At home, you either become the housekeeper, the chef, or the mechanic. If you have kids, you become a parent. When you run your own business you become a leader of your own destiny, and someone capable of leaving a legacy to the world.

You are not a wife/husband when you are in primary one and you are not a pupil when you leave school. You are not a parent until you have children, and you are not considered to be analytical and logical if you are creative.

However, you can be anything you want to be. Each stage of your life and each environment you are in; you will be a different person. Something inside usually stays the same or feels the same but I can guarantee that you act differently when you are with your parents than when you are with your lover or your friends.

This is because one of your four minds will lead the show and believe it knows how best to behave in each situation, and this could also vary depending on your environment. You may be quite body-conscious in a new relationship yet eat and drink to excess when you break up. You could be very spiritual in the morning when you meditate yet when you walk into the office you become very logical, then creative when you are with your friends or playing with your kids. If you are a woman, then you will be very emotional at a certain time of the month and get annoyed at the slightest irritating thing, yet at other times of the month it is something you don't even notice.

Over the years I adopted the identity of the accountant. I am very logical and very analytical. However, a few years ago I found myself being drawn to spiritual and creative activities. I fought with these two identities for a very long time believing that I had to choose one over the other. That was until I realised that they were both part of me and they both had a strength at different times of the day and with different clients. Choosing one over the other would be like saying we love one of our children, or parents, over another.

I found that these two parts when aligned, and talking to one another, gave me an added advantage over other accountants as I understood the work of therapists and coaches. This enabled me to help them grow their business as I had a clear understanding of how they felt and what motivated them. I also had the added advantage of enjoying working with them due to my interest and passion in what they did and the gifts they offered.

A part of us may take the lead in some situations, but all the different identities (e.g. sibling, child, parent, YOU!) that we associate ourselves with like to be heard. If we stay in one identity too long, we may even get lost which is where my mum found herself and where I see many business owners.

My mum told me that she found herself wearing many different identities. She was a wife, a mother, a peacemaker, a victim, a neighbour, a daughter and a waitress. She had no sense of her own identity. She had no idea who Barbara was underneath all those labels. She knew what her husband wanted, she knew what her daughter and son wanted, and what her employer wanted. However, she didn't know what Barbara wanted. Until one day in hospital recovering from an operation, she found herself with the space to ask the question and the time to listen to the answer. Through that process she decided to take charge of her destiny. By doing this she changed her future, she changed my brother's future and she changed my future.

Have the courage to ask what you really want, believe it is possible and be brave enough to reach for it. Bring your team together; ask your head, heart, body and soul what they want and allow the space for the answer to emerge. You may even change your life and the lives of those you care about.

Top takeaway from this chapter:

Your identity is that part of you which is best suited to the environment you are in. If you change your environment, you may just find a different part of you is better suited to lead the way. However, always remember to listen to every part of you. Your head, heart, body and soul are all capable of leading the way, but the successful path is the one that has them all in agreement as to which way to go and which one leads in each situation.

PART 5

*Integration and further resources
(Best Practices, Time Management
and Marketing)*

BEST PRACTICES

By now you will be clear on what you think of money and success and be in the process of updating some programs in your subconscious so they are aligned to what you really want. You may have also identified a self-love deficit and fears that you have and be working towards overcoming these both. You are almost ready to take action that is aligned with your head, heart, body and soul. I have incorporated an agenda checklist at the end of the section and it can also be downloaded from my website: www.hmcoaching.co.uk/successful-business-minds-resources

This section gives suggestions that add to the examples I have given throughout the book. However, please note that although the techniques and tips work for either my clients or I, it is important that you hold a 'Meeting of the Minds' before taking action. The ideas that follow here are to help spark a creative thought for you so you can get curious in your meeting.

Why fairness and values are important

I read an article that discussed why family businesses outperform leading public companies and the underlying factor was simply incorporating fairness into the values of the business.

Each of us run our businesses differently and each of us adopt business practices that fit nicely with our values, but if you are kind, then I believe your business will be successful whether you are a family run business or not.

In my experience I have seen many different business practices (family run or not) and I believe the best to adopt are:

1. Remember that you are always dealing with a person who has feelings and values too (staff, customers and suppliers).
2. Have a holistic view when looking at performance.
3. Have no or very little debt.
4. Have a long term strategy for the business.
5. Have great management skills.

Whichever business practices you adopt, and there will be many people including me advising you which to incorporate, it is important to choose the ones that resonate with you; those that fit the identity of the person you want to be and mirror your values.

There will be times when you are not sure what to do. These are the times when you need to have a meeting of your minds in a nice relaxed state.

A friend of mine wrote the following poem during an emotional moment in her life and after she shared it with me I asked her if I could share it with you. I think this is a very beautiful poem that address that sometimes we just don't know what to do. These are the times we need to go inwards, meditate and have that meeting of our minds.

Sometimes by Linsey Denham

Sometimes it's just too hard to be a grown-up.
Sometimes it feels like the child within is screaming to be in charge.
Sometimes I want to let her win and run and hide and disappear from everyone.
Sometimes I feel so alone in this place that I don't know how I shall survive it.
Sometimes I just want to be able to tell someone how devastated I feel at my lack of courage to face myself.
Sometimes the tears pour like a waterfall and yet the sobs are still stifled because I feel that they make me seem weak.
Sometimes I have no clue how I will turn it all around.
Sometimes I just need to write it down so that I can see it in words and know that I have been here before and that I got through it the last time.
Sometimes though, the pain feels almost unbearable and I wonder why?
Sometimes I just wish I knew that there was a purpose behind it all.
Sometimes I lose the beliefs that usually keep me facing forward.
Sometimes that scared little girl takes over and she is paralysed, sighing and spent.
Sometimes is right now...and I will now meditate in this 'Sometime'

Top takeaway from this chapter:

Choose a business model that works for you. Go inwards and meditate on how you feel in this moment and have a meeting of your minds.

TIME MANAGEMENT AND PRODUCTIVITY

In a recent survey I carried out, 17% said their biggest challenge was time, so I felt that it deserved a chapter too. I completely resonate with this challenge as I'm still looking for that time machine! I thought it would be useful to include some tips and techniques that have been helpful for my clients, and me. Feel free to either adopt or make adjustments and experiment with what works for you.

In *12 Steps to Improve Your Cashflow* I introduced the concept of your physical health being a direct correlation to that of your business health. If you are nourished and healthy then so too is your business. The biggest factor in managing time is understanding that if you neglect yourself, you are also neglecting your business. It is a common misconception that to make the best use of your time you should cram lots into your day. That is not the case.

You are the most important person in your business so make sure you are giving yourself breaks throughout the day, and you are taking time off for holidays. You need to recharge your batteries and only come back to the working day when you are full of energy. It is often thought that the secret to being productive is to work non-stop, but this is not good for you.

Your body and mind regularly needs breaks away from the task in hand. Your mind finds the solutions you strive for when you're doing something else, usually when doing exercise, chatting to someone about their problems or making the dinner! I also encourage you to have plenty of water, good nutritional food and enough sleep so that your mind and body can function at its full capacity. To quote the 1980's Mars advert it really is a balancing act between *'Work Rest, and Play'.*

Whenever I feel overwhelmed it is because I'm telling myself I have to do everything I write on my 'To Do' List. I forget that I am in control of my work, nobody is making me do anything, and therefore I only have myself to ask is this really all necessary?

Whenever I work on something I give it my full attention. For me this means switching off the emails and turning my phone to silent. I always have a notebook next to me to jot down anything that pops into my head; things I think I need to do that are not relevant to the task in hand. I then later question just how necessary these additional tasks are, and if important and will contribute to my success, they get scheduled in my diary to do. I know that may sound boring and it may not work for you, but scheduling in my 'to-do' items means I have a more realistic idea how long it will take to do, rather than just listing 5 things (which always grow throughout the day!) and say I must get them all done today.

I now schedule in twelve months ahead (roughly!) factoring in breaks and leaving a small gap each week to catch up if I have any unexpected hiccups. My assistant laughs at me when she reads my planner and sees that I have my evenings and weekends scheduled with things like personal admin, spend time with my partner, cycle, research, tennis, yoga and meditate. However, these are all things I want to give my attention to and I feel happier doing them so I ensure that I factor them in.

I always make sure I give myself enough time in the morning to wake up and remember what kind of fun things I like doing, and what kind of person I want to be today. I contemplate what I would like to get done in the day ahead and think about whether they contribute to any of my overall intentions. If they do not, then I will explore why I thought I must get this thing done.

I have not always done this and until a short while ago I found myself regularly in a low mood, pushing myself through the day with caffeine and sugar, burning the midnight oil and wishing I didn't have a business at all. I have never openly spoken about this with anyone except my family and mentors, but once when I was quite stressed about running the business, I confided in a long standing client and friend, who gave me a big hug and told me that I had not been looking after myself. She told me that she loved me and that she tells everyone about me, and that another of my clients had been raving to her about me. I took her advice and started looking after myself more. I had a holiday coming up but I cleared out the work I had scheduled for the next few days and brought my holiday forward. I felt much better after the rest and now I am more mindful with my actions and what I eat and drink.

No matter how many books you read and how many people encourage you to do something, it will only happen if you do it. Give it a go and see for yourself just how good it makes you feel and how much time you actually have when you look after yourself, give yourself regular breaks, and only focus on the one thing you really want to do. You can be a business owner, a loving partner/parent/child/sibling/friend, enjoy your hobbies and still run your business and get stuff done. However, this will only happen if you are honest about what you want, make a commitment to do it and be focused when you are doing it.

Remember to assess each task's importance, ask how it will contribute to your business objective today. If after fifteen seconds you are still thinking of a proper argument, ditch it.

How can I find the time to do it all?

Running a business can involve doing a lot of things. You likely find that every time you cross one thing off your 'To Do List' another four things get added on! A lot of business owners struggle with how best to allocate their time and there is no right or wrong answer as everyone is different. I think you must be honest and ask what do you really want from life and how do you want your business to contribute to that? You then apply those goals to the tasks you have on your 'to do' list. I often write key intentions on the top of my weekly planners and 'to do' list to serve as another reminder. This year I have 'Love-Trust-Focus-Patience-Let Go' on every page of my weekly planner for the year. Margaret, my assistant, laughs at my wee notes but they help remind me of my intentions.

In my experience, the more that is written down, the clearer your mind is, as it has less to remember.

There will be distractions

Some people will often choose distractions, usually unconsciously, because they are putting something off. They can fool themselves into believing something else is part of their business objective. Which is why it's useful to tie in each 'To Do' activity with each Intention you have and how that fits in.

Do you remember when you were at school or college and you would start cleaning your room when you were studying for exams? It certainly helped your brain to do an activity and have a clean and clear environment but that was just an excuse. You had many other opportunities to do those activities but you choose your study time to do it in. I had Margaret asking me what I was putting off recently, when she walked in one morning to find me re-arranging the office! I had been putting off editing this book because I had a moment of weakness as I listened to my emotional mind over the others, and gave into my fears. She knows me so well!

Having someone look over your 'To Do' list for the day could be useful too. Often my partner and I share a car as he works close by, and he will ask me what I have planned today. By listing the few things to him I have on my to-do list, it helps me get clear what I need (and want) to do the minute I walk into the office. Occasionally he will ask if an activity is necessary which helps me get clear on whether it is or not.

Do you value your time?

I learned that when I worked on my business, or when I was with a client, friend or family member it was important that I accepted my time and theirs was precious. I give them my full attention but only did the things I wanted to do or that would help them without compromising my own values. At times though I had to be disciplined about what I did, when and for how long especially if there were other things I wanted or had to do. There were, and still are, times when I forget but life usually gives me a gentle reminder.

For example, I had a client who loved going to multiple networking events because he got a buzz out the social side of it, yet he was not following up any leads nor actually getting time to do his work as he was out all the time! In our coaching sessions Jim and I looked at each of the networking events he attended and explored if they fulfilled his business intention and/or did they fulfil his social life. He got clear about the ones that were useful for his business and he acknowledged the ones that he liked going to for the social activities. I encouraged him to keep going to both of these as long as he was mindful of those that were social engagements and not work related. The reason being was that he was saying he was working when he was at these, so then he was taking a morning off the next day to make up for his lost evening 'working'. He was also saying he would help out at the business events as he was a helpful guy and just loved being around people but it took him away from doing his work.

Once he became clear on what intention each event was contributing to, he actually found himself reducing the number he went to and also reducing the amount of work he volunteered to do. Jim then found that he had time to follow up those who had expressed an interest in working with him as well as having the time to service those clients. He still pops along to the social ones too but he no longer fools himself into thinking it is work. He has however got sales from these events because he was being more authentic and relaxed at the social events.

Time is precious to us all so please value your time, ensure others value your time and do what you love doing. Remember if you don't value your time, then you will attract others who don't value your time either.

Switching off and waking up

Remember to give yourself time to wake up in the morning before you start your day. Every morning when you wake up spend a few minutes thinking ahead to later that evening. What will you be happy with having accomplished today? Get a sense of that victory now.

Switch off an hour or two before bed too. It is tempting to stay up late when you are in flow or have a deadline to meet, but it is equally important to switch off your laptop and all electronic devices at least two hours before bed. The blue light on your screens is an LED light that simulates serotonin (a wake up chemical in your brain) instead of melatonin (a sleep chemical). It is also said that melatonin remains activated for twelve hours therefore if you don't switch off until 10pm at night, it is unlikely you will be alert until approximately 10am the next morning.

http://sleepfoundation.org/sleep-topics/melatonin-and-sleep (accessed 21st July 2015).

Be disciplined

Be disciplined enough to stick to your 'To Do' list, only deviating in an emergency. Work out what works best for you. Does a large 'To Do' list work for you or a manageable one? I personally prefer a balance between a large 'to do' list but manageable, assuming everything works out ok! If something happens then be compassionate about not getting everything done on time. I am a member of a few online networking groups and one lady mentioned that she doesn't like being told what to do, even by herself! Therefore she does not have a 'to-do' list. I don't know how effective she is at getting everything done but if it works for her then great. I get like this too but it's usually when I am self-sabotaging my efforts.

When asked for an emergency meeting/appointment if you have space then great but if you don't then say no. Remember you need to rest too. Margaret laughs that I have lunch, dinner and a walk scheduled in my daily planner. I do this because when the cognitive mind is looking at the 'to do' list and working out how it can fit in a last minute request it will only consider what is on the list. It will not be thinking 'Oh what about lunch, dinner or that walk?' but the somatic mind will.

Experiment with what works for you. Be a scientist and be curious.

Make sure you do rest on your days off. Each week I like to have one day where I leave my phone and laptop switched off. The next day I always come back refreshed. Additionally, when you go on holiday stay switched off where possible.

When it is lunch or dinner time, sit elsewhere rather than your work space. Go for a walk or do something different. I often have to force myself to go out in the cold, windy or drizzly Scottish weather but I do enjoy my afternoon walk after lunch. In the evening I would recommend you sit at the table with the TV switched off mainly because I am a great believer in being present with our family/friends and food. Getting away from your work can often give you a different perspective and help you gain focus and energy for what is next on the to-do list.

Be realistic about your time and schedule in emergencies

Bring your deadline forward. Life has a habit of upsetting our plans so don't leave anything to the last minute. I manage a business in addition to studying a second degree with the Open University and writing a book. I have had weeks where I have had tax and accounts deadlines as well as an assignment due in, so I am glad I did some work in advance.

Emergencies, whether business related or personal will happen. However, we can prepare for them. My gran was ill, then later taken to hospital, last year and I wanted to spend time with her but my schedule was jammed packed, primarily because I had promised myself that this book would be out in December 2015! I had to accept that it was not going to happen and that my gran was more important. She is still not well and my planner ensures I go to see her regularly. I now also build in a few hours each week for regular client emergencies for things such as help with accounting or tax related questions. So far all of them have been needed!

I often find that when I am going on holiday the next day, or I have promised a friend I would meet them for lunch or dinner, it spurs me into action because I am conscious of the limited time I have available and I have something exciting to look forward to. I have also noticed that I work far more efficiently in the afternoon and evening so I hold most of my meetings in the morning. For me it is all about working my diary around what I know works and sometimes it is a trial-and-error process.

I recommend that you build in time each week for admin, your finances and marketing. It does not have to be a full day although I do have a few clients that have a designated day that covers their admin, catching up in their finances and doing a little business development or marketing. I prefer to spread these activities out throughout the week though. Just work out what works best for you. If you neglect your admin, accounts and business development then your productivity will be affected.

Be honest about how much time you spend on distractions

I log completely out of all social media sites on my phone or go as far as switching my phone off. It then makes me choose wisely if I have fifteen minutes to spare between meetings to think about the book I am writing, brain storm some ideas or even just sit and be mindful. Additionally, my TV is not linked up to live TV which means I don't get distracted by the popular TV programmes everyone else is watching and talking about. I do get distracted by books though and the odd documentary film on the internet!

Unsubscribe from emailing lists periodically if you are not getting any value from them. The free stuff is great but only if it is what you want. Unless you read them within a few days, print them out, or are saving them for research you will not read them later. I know. I keep thinking this time will be different. A business social media account page is great for scanning the news, updates and any blogs or event announcements you may have missed.

Have your notes all in one place. You could download an app to your phone/ tablet/laptop or use an electronic diary. Alternatively, stick to the traditional notebook and pen but take it from experience having too many options available means you will use them all and everything will be all over the place!

Ignore any emails that are not relevant to the task in hand. You don't have to be available 24/7 nor get back to someone immediately. If you cannot ignore then switch your email server off or the phone off. I suggested removing the notification pop up to a client and she swears it increased her productivity by 100%!

Above all, go easy on yourself

Are you wanting to be more efficient or are wanting to be a super hero? I mentioned at the start of this chapter that I am always looking for a time machine. Two coaches I have worked with have dropped hints that I expect too much of myself. This is something that I'm still fine tuning (I am human after all!) but when I do go easy on myself everything seems to be so much more effortless. Delegate what you can to who you can. That can either be at home or in your business. Ask your partner or kids to help out or get some help at home. Employ someone in your business either part time of full time or get an expert to help you with some tasks.

Have rests (or cat naps as my gran calls them) if you need them. When you are tired acknowledge you are tired and do something about it. I would also suggest reducing any reliance on sugar and caffeine to get you through the day. Sugar is very addictive and it has some interesting side effects when you try and wean yourself off it. Equally though, be compassionate. Water is quite hydrating but it does not hit that same spot! I used to drink three cans of full fat sugary drinks and it was some effort coming off them even with my hypnotherapy and NLP tools. I am glad I managed it but I still occasionally miss that energy boost! I replaced it with doing things I love doing and going for a walk in the fresh air and being compassionate about what I can and cannot do in a day. Alcohol the night before, or even a few days before, can often affect my productivity during the day too. For others this may not be so. I encourage you to be a scientist and explore what is the best mix for you.

On days you are busy, keep the dinners simple like pasta and sauce or pizza. Add vegetables so you get your nutrients. Get takeaway if you have to and can afford to. It does not have to unhealthy and if you are clever with what you buy it can last over two nights.

If you are really busy, focus on what needs done but don't be so focused that you ignore those around you. You need people in your life and you need support. Just ask them to leave you alone for an hour or so if you need it.

Passive Income

Often we work excessive hours to generate the income, as most service work is time related. However, if you can generate passive income in your business then you can have money coming in when you are on holiday or spending time with your partner or kids.

There are various options available to you for passive income and most will require a little investment (cash and time) up front. Examples include offering online courses, eBooks, books, affiliate income by advertising others, selling beauty or health products, or being part of a network marketing scheme.

If you decide to be part of a network marketing scheme, then choose one that is aligned with what you do and/or your values. For example, a friend of mine who is a gas installer and servicer sells Utility Warehouse effortlessly. I tried it as I love their values but it wasn't aligned with my business as well as his. A lady in my network who offers training sells aloe-vera related products as she loves them and can testify to the difference they made to her life. Another lady sells holistic remedies as part of her therapy business.

Top takeaway from this chapter:

Be clear and compassionate about what you can and cannot do. If something isn't working, then change it. Ask what works for others and experiment yourself.
Consider passive income to increase sales that are less reliant on your time. However, remember to ensure your prices reflect the true value you give your customers too.

MARKETING: THE BEST TOOL IN MARKETING IS TO BE YOURSELF

A business book would not be complete without a section on marketing but there are far more insightful books and experts out there on sales and marketing than me. However, I have learnt a few things I would like to share with you. The most important thing to remember when marketing your business is to be yourself.

If you are yourself, you will draw people to you. Seriously it does happen. Obviously you need to be out there talking to people as well as being online. Hiding in your office or clinic is not going to get results even on social media. People want to see you and hear you. Be honest about who you are and what you think. It is a given that the more compassionate you are, the probability that people will like you is high. They want to hear what other people think of you, so gather some personal recommendations and share them. If you do a great job, ask people to tell others about you.

The one thing NOT to do is appear desperate by forcing your product or service on people. Nobody likes it, even if they do need it. It's what they want that matters. They have to want you and your service/product. There are enough customers out there for all of us. Each of us has a different personality and each of us has a different way of providing the service. Trust that the customer that is right for you will find you but that will not happen sitting at home. Get out there. Be honest about what you are passionate about and they will find you.

Do your research

Market research is essential to the success of your business. It is needed when you are starting a business, and it should be reviewed regularly if you have an existing business. It is quite important to spend time thinking about the type of people who would buy your product or service ie the market, and also researching those businesses which are already supplying to that market or supplying to a similar market. Spend the majority of your time giving thought to your ideal customer too.

Personally, I would say, as a general rule, the greater the risk you have of your business failing, the more time you should spend on the market research. It all depends on how successful you want to be in reaching your market who will then buy your products or services and where you can find them.

Be careful though that you don't create a business that is an exact replica of another business supplying to the same market that you are interested in.

Look at your fellow competitors but don't copy them. If you like what they are doing, do it but in a different way. Be original. Listen to your potential/existing customers. Listen to their complaints, their praises and comments. Think 'how can I make their experience better' and trial a few ideas.

Too many businesses do the same thing and it is good for your customers to have more choice. However, if you want a decent share of the market and want your customers to return time and time again, give them a different experience, a much more pleasant experience, than other businesses.

Warm up the cold calls

I am not a fan of receiving cold calls but they can be made a little warmer. Before phoning anyone, do your homework. Research the potential customer's business and their industry before calling. You need to get a feel for how your products and/or services could help them and what challenges they are currently facing. Your products and services maybe fantastic but when talking to anyone you must see it from their perspective. That to me is the art of building any relationship. It will also give you a better indication if they are likely to buy from you or not, and quite frankly rejection is not nice, so do what you can to minimise this where possible.

Remember they are running a business too and that likely means they are too busy to spend ages on the phone or in a meeting whilst you tell them how wonderful your product or service is. Tell them how your service/product can help them. Your sales pitch needs to be tweaked for every customer you call. You need to find out what their biggest problem is and solve it.

Unfortunately, after doing your homework, and getting through to speak to them, you may still not get a sale but at least you can put your hand on your heart and say you gave it your best shot. As long as you have promoted yourself well, and been polite, it may still lead to a sale, just not from them. Remember whoever you speak to, they always know other people. They might have not needed what you had to offer, despite your homework, but they have contacts and friends so you just never know where that call could lead.

However, before you go out and chase new customers ensure your current customers know what products and services you offer. The last thing you want is to chase after new customers then lose your current customer base to someone else because they didn't know everything you have to offer. Also ensure you know just how much work you can take on. What availability you have got and when can you fit them in. If you get too many new customers, you may not be able to service your current ones! This is why I do a twelve-month planner so I know what I can and cannot fit in.

To me, selling is an art and something that must be done with passion, respect and manners. There is nothing worse than taking a call from a sales person who then asks what your business is all about. I have had a sales call where the person asked me what my company was called about five minutes into the conversation! They clearly had just a random mailing list in front of them and had not done their homework. Needless to say I told them where to go!

Your business needs sales, and there are a variety of opportunities available to you. You want to identify who needs what you have to offer, and how to reach them. You just need to choose the quickest, cheapest, effective, yet compassionate approach. There are lots of opportunities, each marketing expert will have their view and each will differ depending on your ideal customer.

Spend time doing a character outline of your ideal customer. It is likely someone very similar to you a few years ago as many business owners go into a business with a service that they felt was not available to them. However, others go into business with a passion and a skill. Identify the person who will buy your product/service. Who will value it and pay the full price. Be specific. Do they have kids, what age are they, what do they spend their money on?

Networking is not about selling

Going to networking events may or may not result in a sale. I personally feel that many people go expecting to sell something. That is not the idea. The idea is to meet people, make friends in business (because it can be lonely) and to tell lots of people about what you do, so that they know about you and can tell others about you if anyone asks them for what you offer. It is about promoting yourself and being seen. It is about getting to know people and making new friends, friends who know what it is like to run a business. You quite likely will get business but when you meet people try to find out about them first, rather than just ploughing straight into your sales pitch!

It is challenging running a business so networking is about making connections and gathering contacts, a bank of people you can recommend to others if asked. It is NOT about getting a list of people to add to your newsletter and to bombard with emails.

In my opinion the best networking events are those which are regular and the same people go to them. That way you get to know about each other. Speed networking is good for being confident and clear about what you do but business usually only tends to get done after a relationship has developed, or they at least find out more about you. That is why it is important to be authentic and meet anyone interested for coffee or offer a free consultation call. The more authentic you are, the more transparent you are and people will see the real you much quicker.

I got quite despondent about networking initially as I felt that I was not able to reply honestly when someone asked 'How's business? And neither was anyone else. I could see it in their body language and the fact they were at every networking event I was at. If you go to too many it is pretty obvious business is not going well, unless of course you have a team of assistants behind you (or you are Jim, a client I mentioned previously who is getting behind with his work). One evening at a networking event, as mentioned earlier, I admitted that business was tough, to a small group of business owners and they too confessed that business was not going too well, minutes after saying it was. We all felt better after being honest and we then spent the rest of the evening coming up with ideas of what to do. That to me is what networking is all about! We are also all quite good friends with one another now.

I would advise that if your time is limited you go to any events where you connect with likeminded people, and perhaps ones where your ideal customer might be, or those who may interact with your ideal customer. Remember your customer may be working excessively and doesn't have time to go to networking events in which case you want to be mixing with their suppliers and their consultants. For example, I have quite a few clients that I never met personally before they contacted me, but their friends, contacts, clients and consultants all told them about me.

Social Media and Websites

Unless your target audience is most definitely not on the internet (my gran for example ...) I would recommend a website. I know some businesses only use a social media account page and whilst I think it is a good start I would always suggest a simple website at least. One of my clients who provides marketing solutions, tells me that the website should be responsive; it should be available via the internet through a pc/laptop, a tablet and a smartphone.

Not all websites can do this and may appear disjointed if the user is looking at it through a tablet or smartphone (which is far more common now). Think about what your website is for before you start spending lots of money building it. If you are selling products on the internet I would advise getting help from a website specialist to ensure that the shop facility is secure.

Marketing via social media, the experts say, should only take thirty minutes each day but in my opinion that depends on how much interaction is taking place and the volume of sales that come from those interactions. It's not productive to be on it half the day either! If you have nothing to say, then there's no point in saying anything, yet equally you shouldn't be afraid to give your opinion on something. It allows people to see what you are passionate about however I would always recommend remaining polite.

I believe there should always be something of value in your post. There is a risk that someone will not see your posts amongst all the others they receive, however repeating the same things continuously throughout the day or week is irritating if your potential customer happens to see it all the time. It's a fine juggling act and there are numerous books, websites, free and paid courses and consultants to help you on how often you post etc. I'm not a marketing expert and I still go to workshops to learn other ways of thinking then apply what I feel comfortable with.

However, I would stress that it all very much depends on who your target audience is and how you wish to communicate with them. There's no right or wrong way, in my opinion. What works for others may not work for you. I believe you must put your own slant on it to really stand out. Interact with current users of your product or services, talk and interact with people, talk about the things your business is passionate about and share your testimonials, but above all just do what feels right for you and your customers.

Top takeaway from this chapter:

**You need to let your ideal customer
know where you are.**

Imagine if you had a problem and it was starting to
frustrate you. Then one day somebody tells you at a
networking event what they do and you realise that
they are that person who can help you! You would
feel pretty happy about that wouldn't you?

Just imagine how happy your customers would be
if they knew about you and the solutions you
could offer them.

HELPFUL BOOKS, MEDITATIONS, ONLINE COURSES AND OTHER RESOURCES

You can access the free meditations and a Meetings of the Mind Agenda by visiting here: http://www.hmcoaching.co.uk/successful-business-minds-resources/

Meeting of the Minds Checklist

What decision or action is being considered?

What does the emotional mind (heart) want to do?
Is the somatic mind (body) capable of doing this? If no, why?
What does the intuitive mind (soul) say or feel about this action/decision?
What does the cognitive mind (head) have to say about this action/decision?

What does the somatic mind (body) want to do?
How does the emotional mind (heart) feel about this action/decision, and why?
What does the intuitive mind (soul) say or feel about this action/decision?
What does the cognitive mind (head) have to say about this action/decision?

What does the intuitive mind (soul) want to do?
How does the emotional mind (heart) feel about this action/decision, and why?
Is the somatic mind (body) capable of doing this? If no, why?
What does the cognitive mind (head) have to say about this action/decision?

What does the cognitive mind (head) want to do?
How does the emotional mind (heart) feel about this action/decision, and why?
Is the somatic mind (body) capable of doing this? If no, why?
What does the intuitive mind (soul) say or feel about this action/decision?

What is the best course of action or decision that is aligned with all four minds?
Are there any behaviours or beliefs that have to be tweaked to help accommodate this? If so, what would they be?
What new behaviours or beliefs would help facilitate this action/decision?

Also please follow me on Twitter at https://twitter.com/hmfinancecoach or on Facebook at https://www.facebook.com/hmcoaching.

I have the following eBooks available from Amazon:
- *12 Steps to Improve Your Cashflow* by Helen Monaghan
- *Understanding the language of your accounts* by Helen Monaghan (due out in August 2016)

I offer 1-1 coaching, finance masterclasses and finance mastermind groups. You can find out more by visiting http://www.hmcoaching.co.uk/services/

I currently provide the following workshops that are based on my books and coaching sessions:
- *Improve your Cashflow* Workshop
- *The Money Mind Paradox* Workshop

You can find out more by visiting http://www.hmcoaching.co.uk/workshops/

Additionally, I recommend the following books. These are all great books that I have read and give the reader great insights & tips into running a successful business and having a successful mindset especially around your finances.

- *Breaking The Habit of Being Yourself* by Joe Dispenza
- *Breakthrough: A Blueprint for Your Mind* by Brian Costello
- *Generatrive Trance* by Stephen Gilligan
- *Heartatude: The 9 Principles of Heart-Centred Success* by Alisoun Mackenzie
- *I Heart Me* by David R. Hamilton
- *Incognito: The Secret Lives of the Brain* by David Eagleman
- *I is for Influence* by Rob Yeung
- *Life Loves You* by Louise Hay & Robert Holden
- *Love Yourself (like your life depends on it)* by Kamal Ravikant
- *Mind Over Money* by Brad Klontz and Ted Klontz
- *Money: A Love Story* by Kate Northrup
- *Money Magnet Mindset* by Marie-Claire Caryle
- *Overcoming Your Underearning* by Barbara Stanny
- *Secrets of the Millionaire Mind* by T Harv Eker
- *Success Intelligence* by Robert Holden
- *The Brain: The Story of You* by David Eagleman
- *The Power of Your Subconscious Mind* by Joseph Murray
- *Think and Grow Rich* by Napoleon Hill
- *Your Book is the Hook* by Karen Williams
  + Any NLP and Psychology Books

I also recommend the following trainers, therapists and coaches to help you with your mindset and grow your business

- Alisoun Mackenzie, Alisoun Ltd – Authenticity and Compassionate Sales
- Aly Townley, Calm Centre - Reiki and NLP
- Avril Gill, Newlands Personal Development – BIH Accredited Hypnotherapy & NLP Training
- Beverley Anderson, BusinessBoostExperts – Solopreneur Business Accelerator
- Brian Costello, Headstrong (Scotland) Ltd – NLP, Hypnosis & Coaching
- Jennifer Falconer, Jennifer Falconer Coaching – Meditation and Life Coaching
- Jill Cruikshank, Leading2Solutions - Business Coach
- Karen Williams, Librotas - Book Mentoring
- Lester Smulski, Transformation-Station – Hypnotherapy
- Linsey Denham, Bach Flower Consults Online – Restoring Emotional Balance
- Lorraine Murray, Connected Kids Ltd – Mindfullness and Meditation
- Mary Thomson, WhiteWater Publishing Ltd – Editing and Publishing
- Michelle Gregory, Gregory Accounting – Associate Chartered Management Accountant
- Sheryl Andrews, Step by Step Listening – Clarity, Confidence & Change
- Susan King, Positive Health – Mind, Body Intelligence